Recovery From Co-dependency

RECOVERY FROM CO-DEPENDENCY:

It's Never Too Late To Reclaim Your Childhood

Laurie Weiss, MA, and
Jonathan B. Weiss, PhD

Health Communications, Inc.
Deerfield Beach, Florida

Laurie Weiss, MA
Jonathan B. Weiss, PhD
Littleton, Colorado

Library of Congress Cataloging-in-Publication Data

Weiss, Laurie
    Recovery from co-dependency : it's never too late to reclaim your
childhood / Laurie Weiss and Jonathan B. Weiss.
        p.   cm.
    Bibliography: p.
    ISBN 0-932194-85-0
    1. Co-dependence (Psychology) 2. Co-dependence (Psychology)-
-Treatment.   I. Weiss, Jonathan B., 1937-   II.Title.
    RC569.5.C63W35   1989   88-28143
    616.86—dc19   CIP

Published by: Health Communications, Inc.
                    3201 S.W. 15th Street
                    Deerfield Beach, Florida 33442

Back Cover Photo by Kai Schuman
Illustrations by R. Kristian Provell

DEDICATION

This book is dedicated to all our teachers: our clients; our parents — Pearl and Jack Ross/Lou and Ray Weiss; our children — Brian Weiss and Linda Rachel Weiss; and to the dedicated professionals who have encouraged our growth.

In addition, we are especially grateful to our manuscript readers for their invaluable suggestions. Jean Illsey Clarke, Larry Gibson, Marian Head, Judy Ruckstuhl, Madonna Snyder and Judy Vaughn left no idea unexamined and no comma unturned in their generous support of this project.

CONTENTS

LIST OF FIGURES

FOREWORD

It is with real pleasure and excitement that I introduce *Recovery From Co-dependency* by Laurie and Jonathan Weiss. Laurie and Jonathan are master therapists and clinicians. They bring their Transactional Analysis (TA) expertise to fruition in this book and they take the current discussion of co-depenency a step further by positing that the crucial issue in co-dependent recovery is connecting with the inner child. It is fitting that they make this move since TA folks have been working with the child part of us from the very beginning.

My specific excitement about this book focuses on two areas. First, it conceptually clarifies in a thorough and useful way the importance of doing inner child work in a developmental context. There is a crucial difference between unmet needs in infancy and unmet needs in the toddler or preschool stages of development. The child in us can be manifested at any stage of development. Each stage has its own needs and energy issues. Each stage must be treated differently from a clinical point of view. This brings me to the second area of excitement about this book.

Jonathan and Laurie have presented some powerful tools for dealing with healing our inner child at each stage of the development process. This, to my knowledge, is an original contribution. I welcome it. It is the approach I have taken for several years in my own inner child workshops. What is useful about this approach is that it allows us a more accurate way to take care of ourselves. Specifically it allows us new awareness. We can see the closed, self-reinforcing system of defense that the inner child sets up in an attempt to adapt and survive. The Weisses give copious examples of this.

Sylvie, in Chapter Three, is ravished with low self-esteem. She is highly judgmental of herself whenever she treats herself as less than perfect. Any problem is taken as proof of her worthlessness. As the Weisses point out, "She responds to the pain of feeling bad about herself by criticizing herself mercilessly for feeling bad, instead of by asking her husband for support and reassurance . . . She even uses the feedback she is getting in therapy as further evidence of how bad she is."

When we understand how we originally learned to cover up our sense of unworthiness, we can use the information to correct our behavior. As adults we can learn new ways of nurturing the specific needs that were never met. For some these may be infancy needs, for others toddler needs, and for others preschool or school age needs. The Weisses bring their rich array of TA tools in offering resources for each level of developmental need. While TA has not used the terminology of the Adult Child movement, it is a therapy model with enormous resources for Adult Children. We owe the Weisses a debt of gratitude for bringing us these powerful resources.

John Bradshaw
Houston, Texas

INTRODUCTION

Abuse, neglect and abandonment of the Inner Child are widespread in our culture; the result is Co-dependence. We generally try to take care of ourselves and get our relational needs met in the same way we were parented, whether that parenting was functional or not. When it was dysfunctional, we tried to anesthetize and repress the pain of our unmet early needs through various addictions and compulsions, and through Co-dependent relationships. We search endlessly for love, for we have never learned to love ourselves.

Love, in the abstract, is not enough for healing the wounds of the Inner Child. Just telling people to love themselves often produces even more frustration and self-criticism in those who would gladly do so if they knew how. This is a "how to" book written to provide specific steps to take that will help readers learn to love themselves.

Love comes in a great variety of forms, flavors and intensities. What is felt as loving is different from one person to another and from one time to another. Furthermore, the Inner Child is not just connected to a single age. What is loving for children of different ages, Inner or Outer, is quite different. In addition, setting appropriate limits, rules and boundaries may not be *experienced* as a loving act by the person being "limited", but may be an essential component of an internal sense of safety in the world.

In our therapeutic work with Adult Children, we have found that it is essential to know what kind of loving is needed at any given moment in the healing process. This information can be ascertained in two ways: first, it is important to *ask* the Inner Child what is needed and to listen carefully to the answers. Second, it is necessary to have a thorough understanding of normal development — a map of the territory covered by the word "needs".

We have drawn on our experience in asking Adult Children what they need in order to heal the damage they experienced as children. From every stage of development, we have learned what kinds of experiences, messages, limits and loving are necessary, and have incorporated them into the resources available to our clients. In this book, we present this information in a form designed to help both the therapist and the Adult Child concerned with his own healing journey.

The first three chapters describe the general problem of Co-dependence, particularly in terms of what issues are likely to be presented to a therapist. Chapters 4 to 7 describe how our basic theoretical framework, Transactional Analysis (TA), can be used to recognize and respond to the most significant of the Adult Child issues, to establish meaningful treatment goals and to design a treatment environment that enhances the healing process.

In Chapter 8, we begin a general discussion of the topic of working with feelings and then present a model for understanding feelings. The discussion is continued in Chapters 12 and 15, where we give more specific information about what to do about anger and grief. We include the discussion of feelings in the part of the book that deals with specific developmental stages, because the appropriate response to a feeling is often determined by the developmental road map.

Chapter 9 describes how developmental problems and the stages they belong to can be diagnosed by observing the difficulties a person encounters in everyday situations. In the subsequent chapters, we turn to a detailed description of each developmental stage. At each stage, we show the relationship between childhood deficits and current adult functioning, and describe the treatment techniques for addressing these deficits.

In the last chapter, we discuss the critical step of deciding to use new information the client has learned in the treatment process. We compare this with the decisions that created the dysfunctional patterns in the first place. We conclude with a discussion of the place of spirituality in the healing process.

This book is written to help end the cycle of child abuse, in which an abused child grows into an Adult Child who passes the abuse on to his own children. Our purpose is to help create a world in which each child is treated with love, honor, respect and appropriate limits.

CHAPTER 1

TREATING CO-DEPENDENCE

Jenny huddles in a corner of the therapy group room with her arms around her knees, trying to be as small as possible. As I approach her, she whimpers, "I feel *bad,* don't touch me, go away!" I reach out to put a hand on her shoulder, and she stiffens and tries to kick me away. I wonder once more how to get through to this badly wounded child — who is 29 years old.

The session began with Jenny complaining that her roommate was ignoring her and withdrawing from her, just as she (Jenny) was beginning to make changes as a result of her therapy. When questioned, she identified that her feelings were similar to those she felt when her mother would leave abruptly when Jenny was four years old.

We suggested that Jenny go ahead and be a four-year-old in the group. She agreed, and picked out a book for me to read to her. As I did so, she said, "I feel bad." I asked where she hurt, and she pointed to her abdomen; I gently rubbed it and told her to breathe deeply; I kept touching her, finished the story, and turned to talk with another client. It was at that point that she suddenly pulled away and retreated to the corner.

I puzzle about the meaning of "I feel bad", and finally realize that Jenny might not be talking about physical pain. I tell her firmly that people aren't for hitting or kicking, and ask, "Do you think you're a bad girl?" That's it! She allows me to touch her and talk. I tell her that she is a fine, ordinary little girl; I don't know of anything she has done that was bad; ordinary children ask for things (like having books read to them); nobody in the room is angry at her and I am happy to be taking care of her.

The words I say to Jenny are quite different from the ones she heard when she was actually four years old, living with a disturbed, paranoid father and an alcoholic mother who would leave unpredictably for weeks at a time. When people talked to Jenny at all, it was often to tell her what a rotten kid she was. She decided that she really was bad, and that it was her badness that caused her mother to leave and her father to beat her. Desperate, frustrated and angry, as a teenager, Jenny turned to drugs and alcohol. Again her feeling of being bad was confirmed. Now, **after six years of sobriety** and several years of psychotherapy, **she is finally ready to deal** with the original hurts experienced in early childhood.

When Jenny began therapy with us two years ago, it was not with the idea in mind that she was there to "heal her *Inner Child* ". She came in because her rigid, compulsive controls over her chemical dependencies were not making her feel any better. Jenny had all of the typical symptoms and problems of someone raised in a dysfunctional family:

1. She was unable to have spontaneous fun.
2. She had severe problems with intimacy.
3. She had an exaggerated need for the approval of others (sometimes covered by a vicious hostility).
4. She was confused about making decisions.
5. She was anxious about making changes.
6. She held rigid, black-and-white judgments.
7. She was afraid of her own anger, and often experienced anger as an outburst of uncontrolled rage, directed at herself or others.
8. She lied and exaggerated at times when it would have been just as easy to tell the truth.
9. She was afraid of abandonment.

10. She tended to associate with and be loyal to needy, damaged people who needed her to take care of them.
11. She had a strong need to control herself and others.

This pattern of problems and symptoms is termed *Co-dependence* by Sharon Wegscheider-Cruse *(Choicemaking)*, and is typical of adults who have grown up in an alcoholic or otherwise dysfunctional family. Such a person may also be referred to as an *Adult Child*, a term which emphasizes the image of a needy child going around in an adult body.

The Inner Child

Jenny is now using the safety of the therapy group to go through the painful process of healing her *Inner Child* — the long-hidden part of herself damaged so severely by the way she was treated as a child.

Most people discover the Inner Child by chance. In the midst of our everyday life, we are catapulted into what Gravitz and Bowden have called "automatic spontaneous age regression". Suddenly we are thinking, feeling and/or acting like a five-year-old (afraid to leave home to go on a business trip), a two-year-old (throwing a screaming temper tantrum when we can't have something we want) or even an infant (being away from someone we love, and feeling that it's a desperate emergency that has to be fixed instantly). **These spontaneous regressions occur when we encounter an experience that is similar in some important way to some emotionally laden childhood event.** The actual event may or may not be remembered consciously, but the feelings associated with the original experience can flood our awareness. We may want to run, hide, giggle or shout as we did (or wanted to) when we were young. We may feel little and powerless, and have great difficulty, momentarily, remembering that we are competent adults.

The Inner Child was originally described by Eric Berne as the *Child Ego State*: a conscious, consistent pattern of thoughts, feelings, attitudes and behaviors that resemble or re-create the experiences a person had as an actual child (Eric Berne, *Transactional Analysis in Psychotherapy, Games People Play*). *Child* is the general term for the part of the personality that experiences needs and emotions. We will use the terms Inner Child and Child (Ego State) synonymously.

Most people have the ability to deliberately turn their attention to the ever-present Inner Child — although they may be reluctant to do so. The process of having a client consciously decide to energize or **cathect** a particular Child Ego State is a central technique in the application of this developmental approach to treatment. Having Jenny cathect her four-year-old Child Ego State allows direct access to the painful experiences of not getting her needs met at that time, and to the healing experience of having someone — the therapist — respond to those needs and feelings in an appropriate way.

We help Jenny cathect her four-year-old Inner Child by providing age-appropriate props, and by *agreeing* to treat her as if she is a four-year-old. We can recognize her Inner Child emerge by watching her behavior. Once given the permission, she spontaneously acts like a real child, expressing her feelings the way a real child would. Although Jenny will never really be four years old again, she *can* experience healthy transactions between her four-year-old Inner Child and a nurturing adult.

Psychotherapy needs to be designed to heal the damage of the wounds suffered by the client as a child, and to recover from the damaging side effects created by the child's inadequate attempts to treat her own wounds.

The process of healing the Inner Child, illustrated, in part, by the work with Jenny, must include the following elements:

1. Recognizing, confronting and interrupting automatic, learned protective behavior patterns (defenses)
2. Feeling and identifying the pain that was created by unmet childhood needs
3. Giving up the fantasy that the pain can be fixed by denying it or by controlling oneself, others, or the environment
4. Grieving, feeling the sadness of losing the magical hope of fixing it
5. Accepting nurturing and information from others
6. Taking action to provide appropriate care for the ongoing needs of the Inner Child

Confronting Current Behavior

The intention of the treatment process is to focus attention on the Inner Child; from this perspective, a current problem can often be confronted as an attempt either to meet the needs of the Inner Child or to defend against the pain of past unmet needs. This is not to say that all current problems must be approached this way. However, when the Adult Child is ineffective at dealing with ordinary life situations, there is probably an unresolved archaic Inner Child issue involved.

When we talk about the "needs of the Inner Child", we are generally referring to essential transactional patterns. When a child is hungry, for example, the important thing, for our purposes, is that the internal state is *expressed* in behavior and is *responded to* appropriately. (This process is discussed in depth in Chapter 4.)

Jenny's problem with her roommate was a predictable result of her association with someone who was needy and dependent, and who would be threatened by Jenny's growth. It was assumed that Jenny's feelings of abandonment (by her roommate) were probably familiar to her. Asking her to find similar feelings from childhood, for example, "How old is the Child that feels that way?" led her to identify that she was approximately four years old when she first encountered those feelings.

These two elements are essential to the healing process, although their order can vary:

1. *Behaving* in a way that provides a healthy transactional experience, comparable to what would have been experienced if the original needs had been met
2. *Feeling the pain* associated with not getting the original needs met

(A more detailed discussion of the transactional needs of a four-year-old can be found in Chapter 14.)

Feeling The Pain

Children who have no environmental support for being themselves and for feeling their feelings find a variety of methods for denying, suppressing and discounting those feelings. (Alice Miller's books, *The Drama of the Gifted Child* and *For Your Own Good*, discuss this concept in detail.)

Like many Adult Children, Jenny is able to report horrible experiences from her childhood in a detached, unemotional fashion. At other times, however, she can be triggered into an intense emotional reaction by some innocuous remark, and is unable to understand why she was so upset. When she was a child, she defended herself against painful experiences by numbing her feelings. She was not aware of the connection between those early experiences and her reactions to her current life situations.

When Jenny allows herself to cathect her Child Ego State, the fear and rage at her abandonment and abuse are remembered and reexperienced, along with the beliefs and decisions she arrived at in an attempt to manage the pain. As Jenny connects the intense feelings with the situations that actually produced them, she is freed to use her adult resources to make new decisions about those experiences. She can then respond appropriately to current problems; she no longer needs to react as if the current situation is the same as the original archaic one. A few weeks after doing this work, Jenny moved into her own apartment.

Giving Up The Fantasy

Young children naturally experience that the world revolves around them. Because they don't understand cause and effect, they can easily come to believe that they are the cause of the things that happen around them. Children normally come to understand the relationship between cause and effect through clear explanations of how things happen. For example, "You didn't *make* your sister hit you. She did that herself, because she was mad at you for taking her toy. You shouldn't have taken it without asking, and she should have done something else about being mad at you for it."

In Jenny's chaotic family, it was impossible to predict what was going to happen next. She tried to make sense of experiences of being beaten, being repeatedly abandoned and being told that she was bad. She was given no accurate information about what made things happen. **Because many of the negative things that happened to her occurred in response to her attempt to get others to respond to her needs, she concluded that the part of her having needs and feelings was bad.** She made up a safe place for herself by creating a fantasy world in which the needy part of her did not exist.

She firmly refused to accept any nurturing from anyone, even when it *was* available, and controlled the approach of others by violent physical rejection. Trying to kick the therapist who was offering nurturing was a re-creation of this behavior.

People become attached to their defensive strategies (fantasies, beliefs) for good reasons. The defenses work, at least to some extent; they manage the pain of not getting the original needs met. Additionally, these defensive patterns contain a paradoxical belief, "If I do this long enough or hard enough or perfectly enough, it will finally fix things and I can then get what I need." They are held in place by hope.

Jenny, like other Adult Children, was reluctant to give up these behaviors, ideas, attitudes and feelings. She held onto the idea that she was bad, and defended it violently, trying to keep out the nurturing that would awaken her hurt Inner Child.

Grieving

Grieving is the process of feeling and expressing the sadness, hurt and anger for the damaging experiences of the past, and for the lack of appropriate nurturing as a young child. Grieving also represents feeling the loss of the fantasy that there is something anyone can do to "fix it".

Grieving a lost childhood is extraordinarily painful. Many people have to face the truth of an entire lifetime of deprivation created by the things they learned to do in order to manage the early pain. It is not surprising that there is often resistance to facing this much pain.

The therapist is often moved to try to comfort and ease the Adult Child's distress, and to prescribe activities designed to help the client feel good. Although this is a useful approach to issues of self-esteem and depression, it is not an effective way to help the client deal with real grief. In such cases, the therapist's role is to acknowledge the reality of the feelings, and to be open and available while the client allows the pain to surface. The therapist who is an Adult Child cannot expect to do this well until he has completed his own grieving.

Grieving can be completed only when the Adult Child recognizes that the past cannot be changed, that the Child can never have the longed-for love in its original, wished-for form. Experiencing this grief frees the Adult Child to invest her energy in healthy attachments and rewarding activities. Jenny is not quite ready to grieve her losses.

Accepting Nurturing

When the archaic Inner Child is awakened, whether spontaneously or deliberately, the desperate, chronic need for nurturing is likely to be experienced. Driven by this powerful, ongoing, unmet, archaic need, Adult Children seek nurturing in their intimate relationships. They unconsciously expect that the partner will be the good parent they never had. However, they are most likely to be attracted to a partner who is similar, in some significant way, to the parent(s) who were unable to meet the needs adequately in the first place. As a result, they often end up proving what they believed to begin with: that the large black hole inside can never be filled and that the needs of the Inner Child can never be satisfied.

Although it is reasonable to expect one's partner to be nurturing, it is not appropriate for that person to provide the corrective parenting needed by the archaic Inner Child. This is an appropriate task for therapy, where the Adult Child can relate to someone who has the necessary knowledge, skill and willingness to accept the parenting role.

In the therapy setting, as in normal healthy parenting, the purpose of nurturing is to support growth and to provide a model for the Adult Child to internalize, so that she develops the ability to take appropriate care of her own Inner Child.

Jenny agreed to be treated as a four-year-old, in order to receive nurturing for her Inner Child. Reading to her triggered both her need for nurturing and her belief that she was bad and in danger because of needing it. The therapist's continued nurturing of the now frightened and upset Child allows Jenny to accept the nurturing more peacefully. Eventually, Jenny incorporates the ability to nurture herself.

Taking Action: Caring For The Inner Child

Learning to recognize the needs, wants and feelings of the Inner Child is an important part of therapy. It often helps to visualize the Inner Child as an actual physical person, who needs to be treated with respect, attention, responsiveness and caring. Looking at a childhood photograph can intensify the visualization.

Asking the Inner Child or the child in the photograph, "What do you need; what would help you to feel better?" may bring internal responses like: "I don't like him! Take me home!" or "I need a hug," "I'm tired, I don't want to do this any more," or "I'm scared he's gonna hit me when he looks like that."

Recognizing and understanding these internal responses is important, but, unless some action is taken in response to them, the Inner Child still ends up being treated as if she doesn't count. **The Adult Child must learn to take action to nurture her own Inner Child on a regular basis.**

The "action" may only be to say to the Inner Child, "I know you are there and that you need something; I will do what I can to see that you get what you need." Doing something about the needs of the Inner Child may mean anything from choosing to rest to choosing to ask someone for strokes to choosing to end a destructive relationship.

Changing behavior involves risk. Because we all have unspoken agreements about how we will act with others, they may react when we change. Jenny's roommate acted angry when Jenny started to nurture her own Inner Child by sometimes sitting quietly and thinking about her needs. Even though Jenny explained why she was acting that way, her roommate remained upset. When Adult Children live in a situation in which denial of the Inner Child is common, reactions like "You're upset over nothing", "You're crazy", "You're being childish" or "You're just a wimp" are common.

The Adult Child needs a safe environment in which the Inner Child can get support for the new, healthy behavior and attitudes. Because her roommate, another Adult Child who isn't yet ready to make her own changes, rejects Jenny, Jenny's first response is to question whether she is doing the right thing. She decides she needs to live alone, rather than be constantly undercut, and turns to her therapy group for support of her new behavior. The group also supports her in experiencing her grief about the loss of her friend.

After she has lived alone for a few weeks, Jenny finds that she has attracted several new friends, who treat her needs for quiet self-contemplation with respect. They even invite her to participate in self-development classes at their church. Jenny accepts and has a wonderful time, using what she learns there to look at new career directions for herself.

The work of healing the Inner Child is not a simple, linear task. It is a complex and convoluted journey of discovery for both client and therapist. It requires the commitment and dedication of everyone involved.

For the therapist, this journey is very much like a commitment to temporarily become a parent to the client's Child Ego State. A certain amount of technical understanding is vital:

1. An understanding of the needs of a developing child, at different ages
2. An understanding of how unmet childhood needs are reflected in adult behavior patterns
3. An understanding of some systematic model of healthy functioning, so that the goal of treatment is clear

Even more important, the therapist must be willing to move beyond a professional detachment and be open to a truly authentic encounter with the client. The therapist needs to be empathic without being overwhelmed and needs to be confrontive without being callous. The therapist needs to be comfortable setting boundaries and limits, must be willing to acknowledge and learn from mistakes and, perhaps the most difficult of all, the therapist needs to model how to honor and take care of his or her own Inner Child.

Clients who undertake this journey must be willing to be active participants in the process, rather than simply presenting themselves for someone to do something to. They need to be willing to face discomfort and feel grief. They need to stop destructive, addictive behaviors and replace them with new, healthy activities. Finally, they must be willing to allow enough time for the Inner Child to learn to trust and to get the nurturing she needs.

The journey is painful, joyful, fearful, intense, powerful, rewarding and exciting. The destination is the sense of health and wholeness that allows joyful and creative participation in life.

CHAPTER

2

Sources of Co-dependence

We watch a mother and grandmother systematically teaching a year-old baby the rudiments of Co-dependence. Cheryl sits on a pillow while her mother, Mia, and her grandmother, Billie, take turns amusing her by handing her different toys. Each time Cheryl reaches for something, one of them hands her something different. If Cheryl holds a toy that mother has given her and seems interested in it, then grandmother replaces the toy with one she thinks will be even more interesting.

A subtle competition for the baby's approval ensues. Cheryl happily accepts whatever is handed to her. She smiles and coos at the attention, but never succeeds in picking up or dropping a toy on her own initiative.

She should be **learning to match her internal experience of wanting something with her own ability to seek it out and learn about it.** Instead, Cheryl is learning to be a toy for her mother and grandmother.

11

Mother and grandmother have good intentions. They want the best for Cheryl — that is one reason they spend so much time playing with her. They each learned their own Co-dependent behaviors under much harsher circumstances. When Mia (at 20, a single parent and a recovering drug addict) was small, Billie was diagnosed as schizophrenic, and was only marginally available to her daughter. Mia learned to ignore most of her own needs and be a good toy for Billie. That way, at least Billie focused some of her wandering attention on Mia.

Billie, now 43, was brutalized when she was a child. She had to shut down almost all awareness of her own needs in infancy. If she made demands for attention, they were responded to with violence. Billie never developed a secure sense of who she was, and was never sure of the boundaries between herself and her world.

When Mia was born, Billie formed such a tight bond with her that she was unable to appreciate that Mia was a separate individual, with her own needs and feelings. She perceived Mia as a part of herself. When Mia expressed needs by normal crying, Billie heard her own crying Inner Child, and was terrified by it. She responded by shutting down and going into a different room or turning on music, so that she wouldn't hear the cries. To Billie's confused Inner Child, who couldn't distinguish between present and past, internal and external, the sound of crying meant getting beaten.

Mia learned at a very young age that if she cried, she would be ignored. She learned instead to be very responsive to Billie whenever Billie expressed any interest in her. She learned to perform whatever behaviors Billie would respond to. She learned the lessons a child of a dysfunctional family must learn — do what it takes to get whatever attention is available. She learned the essence of Co-dependence.

Learning To Deny

The growing child learns how to get sufficient nurturing to survive and grow. Co-dependent behavior patterns develop when the caretaker is too upset with her own problems, whatever they may be, to be available for appropriate nurturing. In that case, the child winds up in the position of having to discount, suppress or deny his own needs and feelings, in favor of those of the caretaker. It is as if the parent says, "I can't stand it (for you to have these needs, make these demands, etc.)!" The child's instinct to survive leads him to a paradoxical decision: "Since you can't stand it, I will take care of you by making it disappear; then you won't be upset and can take care of me."

A child who learns to deny his own needs in order to obtain limited care can never really escape the pain that comes with the absence of real nurturing — nurturing that is responsive to the child's own needs. As the child grows to adulthood, he becomes an Adult Child, and the pain remains with the forgotten Inner Child.

Nobody has perfect parents; and nobody *is* a perfect parent. Therefore, we all grow up with some unresolved pain in the Inner Child part of ourselves. We all deny some needs and have some of the behavior traits of Adult Children. Co-dependent behaviors, like the unmet needs that caused them, exist on a continuum of intensity and severity. Even people who grew up in relatively healthy environments exhibit some of the traits. Adult Children, attempting to adapt to dysfunctional environments, may believe that their very survival depends on rigidly obeying the basic family rules of "Don't Trust", "Don't Talk" and "Don't Feel" as described by Claudia Black in *It Will Never Happen To Me.*

Definitions Of Co-dependence

Some authors see Co-dependence as an almost universal disease of our culture (see Anne Wilson Schaef, *Co-Dependence: Misunderstood, Mistreated* and *When Society Is An Addict,* and Robin Norwood, *Women Who Love Too Much,* for examples of this point of view).

Robert Subby, in *Co-dependency: An Emerging Issue,* defined Co-dependence as, "An emotional, psychological and behavioral condition that develops as a result of an individual's prolonged exposure to, and practice of, a set of oppressive rules — rules which prevent the open expression of feeling as well as the direct discussion of personal and interpersonal problems."

Sharon Wegscheider-Cruse describes Co-dependence as "a normal response to an abnormal situation" characterized by denial, compulsive behavior, frozen feelings and behavioral stuckness (*Choicemaking*).

Timmen Cermak, in *Diagnosing and Treating Co-dependence,* defines Co-dependence as a personality disorder. He distinguishes between the familiar Co-dependent traits and identifiable dysfunctions resulting from excessive rigidity or intensity associated with these traits.

Factors Affecting Severity

The extent of damage to the Inner Child depends on a variety
of factors:

Age Of Child At Time Needs Were Not Met

A hungry infant does not have many alternatives, if he is not
responded to when he cries. He can cry louder or longer, or he
can stop crying. A hungry four-year-old, in contrast, can ask for
what he wants, can ask for a variety of different things, can ask
different people and can also get the food himself. Because all
developmental learning is based on earlier development, the
younger the child, the more the damage may affect subsequent
development.

Relative Harshness Of Environment

Mia's needs were just not responded to; Billie was actively
mistreated when she expressed her needs.

Availability Of Alternate Sources Of Nurturing

Many children have siblings, extended family, friends, teachers
or neighbors they can turn to for comfort and nurturing if things
get too tough at home. Some, however, may be more isolated or
may feel compelled to stay in the situation in order to protect the
mother or the other children from abuse.

Cultural Support For Mistreatment

Alice Miller's remarkable books, *For Your Own Good* and *The
Drama of the Gifted Child*, vividly describe child-rearing practices
and values that have been widely accepted as common practice in
Germany for the last 200 years. Many of these practices, explicitly
designed to break the will of the child, would today be considered
emotional child abuse.

Genetic, Physiological And Constitutional
Characteristics Of The Child

Each child has his own unique, biologically based pattern of
responsiveness. Differences in general activity level, pain thresholds,
maturation rates and other important factors can dramatically shape

a child's reaction to behavioral and psychological influences.

Birth Order And Family Constellation

It is clear that different children in a family do not live in exactly the same world; one has an older brother, another has a younger sister, etc. In *The Birth Order Book,* Kevin Leman describes some of the research findings on the effects of birth order on personality.

In this context, the effect of the family roles described by Wegscheider-Cruse can be considered; life is very different for the Scapegoat than for the Family Hero, for example.

Amount Of Denial Present In The Family

When problems are acknowledged realistically, it is much easier for a child to learn healthy ways of handling them. The mother who says, "Daddy's camping," when the father is passed out drunk on the front lawn (related by Claudia Black), is seriously interfering with the child's ability to make sense of his reality.

Child's Sense Of Control Of Environment

Studies of learned helplessness show that individuals who believe (whether correctly or not) that they have some control of their situation have higher self-esteem than those who believe they are helpless (Blair Justice, *Who Gets Sick?*).

Effects Of The Damage

The Adult Child attempts to manage the pain of the Inner Child by adopting a variety of more-or-less dysfunctional patterns. The growing literature on the problems of Adult Children of Alcoholics and other dysfunctional families is a kind of damage report on the results. Everything from the use of addictive chemicals to paranoid avoidance; from always being sweet and nice to being domineering and controlling; from avoiding all intimacy to clinging desperately to anyone available — these varied strategies are beginning to be understood as methods of attempting to manage the pain of the Inner Child.

Unfortunately, many of these strategies succeed only in creating additional problems. They become an additional source of pain, on top of the original pain from childhood. Because the new problems are more immediate and obvious than the suppressed archaic ones, the new ones become the focus of the Adult Child's attention.

These problems can be controlled, but they are basically symptoms, and cannot be truly healed until the pain of the Inner Child is addressed. All the problems arise because of the unmet needs of the Inner Child — unmet because the parents are themselves Adult Children. They can rarely give their children the healthy parenting they didn't receive themselves.

Breaking The Cycle

Co-dependence will continue to be passed from generation to generation until this cycle of deprivation and inappropriate parenting can be interrupted. When we treat the Inner Child by providing corrective parenting experiences, the Adult Child can then give the children of the next generation the appropriate parenting they need in order to grow up healthy.

Because *Mia* and *Billie* are in treatment together, we decided to teach them new parenting skills so that *Cheryl* can get appropriate care now. We explain that Cheryl needs space to explore her own environment, and that she needs to know they are still available to her while she does this. We suggest that they let Cheryl do her exploration in a room where they are doing other activities, and can make sure she is safe and can smile at her from time to time.

As they receive the information about Cheryl's needs, Billie and Mia begin to recognize their own deficiencies. We suggest to them that they can use the group therapy setting to experience a safe setting in which to explore their own environments, based on their own initiative. Cheryl, at least, won't teach these Co-dependent patterns to her children.

We believe that the motivation for Co-dependent behavior can be greatly reduced when the unmet needs at specific developmental stages are identified and treated with corrective parenting. We will discuss how to recognize these needs and what to do about them in subsequent chapters.

CHAPTER 3

CENTRAL ISSUES IN TREATMENT

Callie is struggling to keep from driving her husband away. Each time he goes on a job interview, she fears that he will never return. She grits her teeth and tries to keep her rising anxiety under control. She knows that the more she clings to him, the more likely he is to want to leave her, but she can't seem to stop herself from begging him not to leave.

Up until now, Callie has been able to keep her fear of abandonment under control, because she has been clinging to the relationship with her infant daughter. At two, however, the daughter is starting the normal developmental process of separating from her mother. With this attachment weakening, Callie's old fears of abandonment come to the surface. She tries to handle them by clinging to her husband.

When I ask Callie about other times in her life when she felt abandoned, she tells me of a mother, addicted to drugs and alcohol, who repeatedly left seven-year-old Callie alone to take care of her three-year-old brother. Mother would disappear for several days at a time, leaving Callie with the warning that she (Mother) might die each time she left. While Mother was gone, Callie would feel panic, but continue to care for herself and her brother. When Callie was eight, she witnessed her mother being badly injured in an accident, and felt guilty that she hadn't taken good enough care of Mother.

Callie told this story without emotion. When I asked if she felt like a little girl when her husband left on routine business, she admitted that she did. I suggested to Callie that her Inner Child was afraid that she would have the same experience with her nurturing husband that she had with her mother. Callie's response was to cry hopelessly, saying that she didn't deserve to be taken care of, because she had not adequately cared for her mother. She "knew" she deserved to be abandoned, and was certain that it would happen again.

Sylvie, recently married, feels insecure, inadequate and jealous when her husband shows the slightest awareness of any other woman. She gets upset when she encounters his old *Playboy* magazines, when he mentions an old girlfriend in passing or when she sees him glance at an attractive woman. **She is extremely critical of herself for having these reactions,** and comes to therapy in order to "get rid of" the part of her that has such feelings.

After a few sessions, Sylvie reports that she understands more about what she is doing, but the problem is worse. She is now going out of her way to search for evidence that her husband is more interested in other women than he is in her. She is so sarcastic, critical and obnoxious about it that he is beginning to lie to her to keep her from getting upset about meaningless events.

The key to the problem **is her low self-esteem, demonstrated by the highly judgmental way she treats herself whenever she is less than perfect.** She is operating in a closed, self-reinforcing system, in which she feels so insecure and inadequate that any problem is taken as proof of her worthlessness. She responds to the pain of feeling bad about herself by criticizing herself mercilessly for feeling bad, instead of by asking her husband for support and reassurance. She stays stuck by criticizing herself for being stuck.

She even uses the feedback she is getting in therapy as further evidence of how bad she is. She is not using the information either to correct what she is doing or to search in her childhood for the answer to how she learned to treat herself so badly. Pointing this out to her only seems to reinforce it.

These examples illustrate some characteristic problems in the treatment of Adult Children. Self-reinforcing belief systems, originally created as a way to manage pain, become barriers that keep the Adult Child from knowing what she needs, or needs to do, in order to break out of the Co-dependent behavior pattern. We will discuss these problems in some detail here, and will describe methods for overcoming them in subsequent chapters.

Foundations For Co-dependent Behavior And Thinking

The foundations for Co-dependent behavior and thinking can occur so early in development that Adult Children don't remember them.

In dysfunctional families, the parents are often Adult Children themselves, and take care of children with inadequate information and skills. Children in dysfunctional families learn to adapt to the feelings of their parents instead of attending to the ordinary tasks of childhood. This becomes the "natural" way to behave. This behavior ensures enough caretaking for survival.

Baby Cheryl (in Chapter 2) was learning not to pay attention to what she wanted herself, and instead to respond to the desires of her mother and grandmother. Cheryl, as an Adult Child, could be expected to have trouble identifying what she needs, and it is unlikely that she would have any memory of how she had learned to discount herself.

When *Nikki* is asked to tell another person, in group, about what she wants, she reacts with terror. She "knows" that something terrible will happen if she does; her Inner Child can't distinguish between knowing and remembering, between "then" and "now". The Inner Child has taken over, to insure her survival in a dangerous world that was real thirty years ago. The Adult Child struggles to deal with current life realities through this "automatic spontaneous age regression".

Extreme Pain Of Early Experiences Leading To Co-dependency

The early experiences that lead to the Co-dependent pattern are usually extremely painful; tremendous energy is expended to maintain denial systems that help to avoid remembering and feeling the pain.

Many Adult Children who come for treatment ask for help in controlling their current behavior. When asked about childhood experiences, they often report that childhood was a relatively happy time. They grew up in an ordinary family; perhaps Dad drank a little too much, but things were generally okay.

Frank asked us to help him maintain his resolve to leave his unresponsive wife. He remembered an "ordinary" childhood, until a probing question suddenly brought back the memory of his terror at listening to the violent arguments between his parents. As we get to know him better, we find that his wife's "unresponsiveness" means that **she doesn't read his mind when he is afraid to ask directly for what he wants.** When he was small, asking for something might have set off one of his father's violent outbursts.

Nikki, too, remembered an ordinary childhood — marred "only" by repeated hospitalizations for stomach trouble. She only came to treatment at all because her physician told her that her continuing stomach problem was psychosomatic.

When the memories of painful early experiences are finally retrieved, other family members may become very upset and try to maintain the denial system.

Bill's mother berates him for "spreading the ugly rumor" that his (long dead) father was an alcoholic.

Roxy's sister won't even talk to her any more, because Roxy began to recall incidents when they both were physically abused.

Remembering past pain, even for the purpose of healing it, can lead to so much current pain that the Adult Child may try to rebury the past.

Even in situations where the Adult Child can answer the question of what she needs, the question of what needs to be done about it runs into another set of barriers.

Early Decisions To Accept Responsibility For Family Difficulties

Adult Children made decisions when they were very young that they were responsible for difficulties in the family. They punish themselves for "causing" these difficulties by rigidly controlling or abusing the Inner Child. As a result, the Inner Child perceives himself to be inadequate or bad. From the viewpoint of the Inner Child, the awareness of a problem or a need is a signal for blame and criticism, not for problem-solving.

Callie believes that she deserves to be abandoned because she "allowed" her mother to be hurt.

Jenny (as many other Adult Children) believes that her Inner Child is bad because she feels angry and needs nurturing.

Marjie believes that she deserves to be beaten by her abusive husband, because she didn't have dinner ready on time.

Ken continually berates himself for being imperfect — a very common Adult Child trait.

Difficulty In Problem-Solving About Getting Needs Met

Problem-solving about getting needs met is difficult because, for many Adult Children, their feelings, beliefs and attitudes are fundamental to their distorted perception of reality. Trying to talk about them is like trying to discuss water with a fish.

Bertha believed that it was useless, impossible and probably dangerous to ask an authority figure to alter anything. As a child, she had learned to adapt to her father and older brothers — to avoid repeated physical and sexual abuse. As an adult, she would either agree to everything anyone (including her therapists) asked her to do or she would go away. She tried to agree with everything she *imagined* that we wanted her to do, despite repeated invitations to state her own desires.

We told her repeatedly that she could choose group or individual treatment, explaining the advantages and disadvantages of each. When she chose group, we invited her to continue individual sessions. She did for a time and then chose to attend only group. She abruptly terminated her treatment with a phone call; she said that group wasn't working for her, and, since *we* wouldn't see her individually, she had switched to a new therapist who would.

Bea told us that her favorite cousin and lifelong confidant had been extremely critical and insulting toward her. When we asked how she felt about the situation, she told us stories about his past, wondered why his alcoholism was getting worse and told us about how much stress he had in his life. She would not talk about her own feelings. The question seemed meaningless to her, although we asked it repeatedly, in several different forms.

Colin believes that he should know how to do anything he

attempts, even when he has had no opportunity to learn. If he makes a mistake, he hides it, believing that his employer will be angry at him for his incompetence. His employer repeatedly asks how things are going, does he understand, does he need help? He lies and maintains that everything is just fine. When he can no longer appear in control, he quits his job, leaving his employer to discover the shambles he leaves behind.

Co-dependency Behavior Defined As Normal

A large proportion of the behavior that keeps the Co-dependent system in place is defined by others as normal and is reinforced by ordinary social expectations.

Because many Adult Children vow to create better families than the one they grew up in, they search for models of how a family is "supposed to be". If they are lucky, they may observe a healthy family in the home of a friend. More often they take models from television programs, movies, popular songs, romantic novels, sports figures and advertisements.

These models are unrealistic, at best. They show that all problems can be solved in two hours or less. They imply that life is constant drama and excitement; calmness is boring.

Many books and songs are about the pain of trying to manage a Co-dependent relationship. If people in love can't read each other's minds, it must not be true love. Many of these models tend to reinforce the low self-esteem of the Adult Child who is trying to do an impossible task perfectly. Because the Adult Child frequently relates to other Adult Children, these misconceptions are shared and mutually reinforced.

Susan single-handedly nursed her dying mother for many weeks. When she finally admitted that she needed help, she considered it to be a sign of weakness, and so did the rest of her dysfunctional family, who criticized her for being "selfish".

Connie's husband praised her when she devoted herself to him and to their children. If she wanted to take a class for her own growth and enjoyment, he became angry and critical, and she felt guilty.

Mike's friends were impressed by his new girlfriend; she cared so much about him that she called him six times each day to keep tabs on him. She treated him with such "devotion" that they tried to persuade him to stay with her, even though he felt stifled.

Any of these central issues can interfere with the process of therapy in a variety of ways. At one extreme, they can be basically simple issues that can be handled easily just by calling them to the client's attention. At the other extreme, they can obscure the client's perspective so much that effective treatment becomes extremely difficult. In either case, it is important for the therapist to deal with these issues in a way that affirms the client's self-respect. The client would not be doing these things in the first place if she were not convinced they were vital to her well-being, and will only change them when she can see a more rewarding alternative.

CHAPTER 4

A SYSTEMATIC TREATMENT APPROACH — PART 1, FOUNDATIONS

Co-dependent behaviors are powerfully motivated and strongly supported by others. To treat them effectively requires an approach that is equally powerful and supportive. The motivation and rewards for progress must be strong enough to offset the pain that is likely to be encountered in the process.

Effective therapy should provide both therapist *and client* with a clear understanding of the mechanisms that create the Co-dependent behaviors and hold them in place. This understanding is facilitated by using a language and concepts that are both understandable for the client and complete enough for the therapist to use for diagnosis and treatment planning. We have found that *Transactional Analysis* (TA) serves this purpose well, and we will illustrate how TA concepts can be used to communicate effectively with clients.

A Healthy Model

The first element of a systematic approach to the treatment of Co-dependence is a model of what a "healthy" person would look like. Having a model of health gives both client and therapist a target to aim for. It also helps to counteract the natural tendency to pay attention only to the things that are not working.

Our working description of a "healthy" person is someone who is aware of his needs and feelings and who takes initiative to do something effective about them. He does this by taking into account: (1) his own needs and feelings, (2) the needs and feelings of others who would be affected by his behavior and (3) the realities of the situation in which the behavior occurs.

This model is based on the idea that whatever is going on "inside" a person — feelings, needs, memories, conflicts, ideas, desires, etc. — will be expressed, sooner or later, in observable behavior. More specifically, it will be seen in actual transactions with other people. Given a way of describing "healthy" behavior, we can then recognize behavior patterns that leave out or distort one or more of the key elements. Because a significant amount of Co-dependent behavior is seen as "normal" by many people, it is necessary to have a clear way to point out to the client what the problem is with any particular pattern.

Transactional Analysis provides a succinct way of stating the healthy model. Briefly, TA describes three major parts to the personality:

1. The *Parent Ego State* is the part that contains the rules, the values and the nurturing and controlling behavior patterns that we learned from our parents and other authority figures.
2. The *Adult Ego State* is the rational, problem-solving part of the personality; its function is to gather, process and report information and to make probability estimates based on the informaton.
3. The *Child Ego State* has been described earlier (see Chapter 1) as the part of the personality with the feelings and emotions; it is synonymous with the Inner Child.

The following diagram is used to represent the three Ego States in the personality:

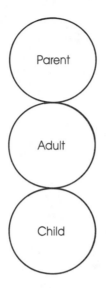

Figure 4.1. Ego States

Using these basic terms, healthy functioning can be described as the person using his Adult to gather information about: (1) what his Child needs and feels, (2) what the other person's Child needs and feels and (3) what the reality of the situation is. The function of the Parent is to give permission to the Inner Child to use the Adult for problem-solving, rather than having to follow specific rules.

An example will clarify these ideas:

If a person wants to see a particular movie (Child), and wants company (Child), he says, "I would like to see the new Rambo film (Adult reporting about Child). Would you like to go with me (Adult question about the other's Child)?"

If the answer is *no*, there are several choices, depending on what is important to the person; all of the choices involve using Adult and Child together. If it is the particular movie that is his most important consideration, he may decide to go alone, or to ask someone else. If the other person's company is the most important factor, he might offer some extra inducement to the other person, negotitate to see a different movie, or do something else entirely, as long as it involved being with the other person.

If they do decide to go out, there will be a discussion about schedules, arrangements, transportation, babysitting and anything else that needs to be taken into account. This is the Adult discussion about the reality of the situation.

If he doesn't see the movie he originally wanted, he either arranges to see it another time or decides it's not important enough to bother with. Regardless of the outcome, all of the negotiation and problem-solving would be done from the position that the desires of both people are okay.

An Adult Child, raised in a dysfunctional family, does not learn such a direct (Adult) system for getting what he wants or needs. Typically, he learns, as a set of Parent rules, that the needs and feelings of other people are the most important thing to pay attention to and that his own needs and feelings are irrelevant. The reality of the situation may or may not be considered; if it is, it will be considered *more important* than his needs and feelings. In this situation, the Adult Child does not learn to use his Adult for its natural purpose, ie., to help his Child figure out how to get what he wants or needs.

As a result, the Adult Child usually hopes that the other person will know what he needs and produce it for him (without his having to run the risk of asking directly for anything). This seldom happens, and, when it does, it only serves to reinforce the Co-dependent patterns.

When an Adult Child wants to see a particular movie with another person, he first tests the atmosphere in an offhand way, saying, "Would you like to go to a movie?" The Child motive is hidden under the seemingly Adult question.

If the answer is *no,* that is the end of the overt exchange; the person does without, but is likely to store some negative feelings in his Child. If the answer is *yes,* the next question is, "What would you like to see?" Again, there is no statement about his own preference. If the other person chooses a different movie, the Adult Child will settle for that, without comment, and may hardly be aware of the disappointment or anger.

Transactional Analysis

Transactional Analysis is a system of understanding human behavior first proposed by Eric Berne in the early 1960s, in *Transactional Analysis in Psychotherapy,* and later popularized in his *Games People Play* and in Thomas Harris' *I'm OK — You're OK.*

The initial popularity of TA was based on the fact that **Berne used simple, colloquial terms to describe the complexities of human motivation and interaction. Berne's position was that a client in psychotherapy was entitled to understand his own problems as clearly as the therapist did** — a radical notion, at the time. Berne's work was meant to demystify psychotherapy, as well as to provide new and more powerful tools and concepts for the process.

Berne's most fundamental contribution was to emphasize the concept of Ego States. He defined an Ego State as "a (coherent) system of feelings accompanied by a related set of behavior patterns." Each person can be seen to have three such patterns, known as the Parent, Adult and Child Ego States. These parts of the personality can be identified by observing the patterns of words, gestures, voice quality, behavior, feelings, attitudes and beliefs. These patterns can be observed by a person about himself, so that the information can be used for self-understanding. The information can also be seen by another person observing the subject, making it useful for a therapist. The operation of Ego States can also be inferred by observing how others tend to respond to a particular pattern of behavior.

The Parent Ego State

The Parent Ego State is originally introjected in whole or in part from our parents and other authority figures. Later, one's own decisions, peer opinions and life experiences can be added to the Parent. The Parent can be observed in operation when an individual attempts to nurture, control, guide or direct himself and others. When a person is "in his Parent", he is using the methods, values, rules, attitudes and behavior patterns he learned from others. These may or may not be useful for current problem-solving.

The Parent in operation can often be described as either nurturing or critical, depending on the attitude conveyed. The content of the Parent ranges from trivial social habits, eg., "You have to wear a belt with your pants," to the most general definitions of character and reality, eg., "You'll never amount to anything; you're a bum, just like your father!"

His own Parent Ego State is the source of most of the negative self-talk experienced by the Adult Child. It repeats internally the criticisms and judgments the Adult Child heard when he was small, often using the same words:

1. "You're stupid!"
2. "You're selfish!"
3. "You should know how to . . ."
4. "Who do you think you are?"
5. "Your feelings are crazy!"
6. "You shouldn't trust . . ."
7. "You'd be better off dead."
8. "You have to take care of . . ."
9. "Hurry up and grow up!"
10. "You shouldn't feel . . ., etc."

These negative messages are sometimes repeated to others, especially young children.

Healthy grown-ups have Parent Ego States that contain messages like:

1. "You can do it!"
2. "You're a good person!"
3. "Don't hurt people."
4. "You belong here!"
5. "Take good care of yourself."
6. "Ask for help when you need it."
7. "Everyone is important."
8. "Share."
9. "Think about it."
10. "Feelings are important, etc."

The Parent Ego State provides structure and direction for the person: it defines what is important to pay attention to, and provides guidelines for setting priorities.

Healthy, positive and life-enhancing Parent messages are learned when a child is nurtured appropriately, in response to his own needs. These messages, too, are likely to be passed on to others.

The Child Ego State

The Child Ego State, or Inner Child, is the part of the personality that experiences and stores emotional experiences, past and present. It is the part of us that feels, needs, wants, laughs, cries, etc. It has the capacity to experience both current and archaic feelings at the same time — sometimes getting them confused, because they are often connected to each other.

Ellie is nervous, uncomfortable and confused (current Child feelings) about confronting a professional colleague about his inappropriate handling of a mutual client. As she talks over the situation in my office, she easily gets into her Adult about the situation, and clearly thinks through what needs to be done and how she will handle it — including what she will do if he doesn't respond to her. After observing her own process, she says, "Why is it so much clearer and easier now than when it first came up?"

On further reflection, she recognizes her initial Child feelings as being the same as those she felt as a little girl, when disagreeing with her father would result in severe criticism and rejection. As she allows herself to remember and reexperience those archaic feelings, she becomes aware of her repressed anger at this treatment, and expresses and releases those angry feelings. When she is through, she understands how the anger at her colleague's behavior stirred up the archaic anger at her father. Because neither anger was permitted by her Parent, she substituted a more familiar and safer Child response.

The Child also stores the patterns of behavior we learned when we were discovering what we could do to get our caretakers to respond to our needs. In response to our experience of the way we were treated, we made decisions about ourselves, others and the way the world probably works. These decisions, and the kinds of activities we undertake in order to carry them out, are described in detail in the Transactional Analysis literature on the concept of *Life Script.* Steiner's *Scripts People Live* and Berne's *What Do You Say After You Say Hello?* are the major resources for this material.

Although we generally speak of "the" Child, as if there is just one, it makes sense to think of there being a connected series of "Children", each of a different age. Thus, the infant part of the Child may feel like being held, whereas the two-year-old wants to be rebellious and the four-year-old wants to ask questions, etc. This point is particularly important when designing interventions; what is appropriate to say to a two-year-old Inner Child is quite different than what needs to be said to an eight-year-old Inner Child.

The Inner Child of the Adult Child often contains decisions and conclusions such as:

1. "I won't trust anyone."
2. "I won't show feelings."
3. "I won't talk about my needs or problems."

4. "I won't ask for anything."
5. "I'm not important."
6. "I'm bad."
7. "I don't count."
8. "I'm supposed to know everything."
9. "I better do it right."
10. "I'll be good."
11. "I can't do anything right, etc."

These survival conclusions are activated by hearing the negative self-talk of the Parent, by internal stressors, such as illness, or by external experiences that are similar to those under which the child made the original limiting decisions.

When the Child is activated, the grown-up behaves or feels as if he is once again a small child (the "automatic spontaneous age regression"). He may act helpless, confused, victimized, whining, belligerent, stoic ("Boys don't cry"), frightened, upset, angry, sad, depressed, guilty, etc.

The Child of the healthy grown-up has had a very different life, and stores experiences of joy, satisfaction, sadness, competence, encouragement, etc. He concludes "I can do it, I'm loved, I'm lovable, I'm important and so are others, I'm capable, etc." When these feelings and decisions are activated, the person appears alive, alert, spontaneous and present.

This is not to say that the Child of a healthy person never experiences negative feelings or emotions. When he does, however, he responds to the feelings as signals that he needs something, and takes initiative to get it (the *healthy model*).

Of course, no one is either completely healthy or completely Co-dependent. These feelings and behaviors exist on a continuum. Adult Children usually function toward the negative end of the continuum, with excursions toward the positive end. Healthy adults usually function in the positive zone, with occasional negative experiences.

The Adult Ego State

The Adult Ego State is a tool for information processing, storage and retrieval, and for predicting the probability of various outcomes. The Adult can observe Parent rules and values without necessarily being run by them, eg., "I know I should go to work, but what would actually happen if I didn't go in today?" In the same way, the Adult can observe Child feelings without being directed by them, eg., "I don't want to complain to my boss, because I'm scared of him. But how else am I going to get the problem solved? Besides, what do I know about how he handles this kind of situation?"

Similarly, the Adult can have access to information about external reality, including the information about the Parent, Adult and Child aspects of other people. The Adult is especially useful as a tool for communication with others. It can report information in a neutral, nonjudgmental and nonemotional manner. Ideally, the Adult can mediate internally between the needs and wants of the Child and the rules of the Parent, reaching a conclusion that accounts for all relevant factors.

Like a computer, the difference between what information the Adult *does* process and what it is *capable* of processing is determined by the programming that runs it. There may be Parent rules about the use of the Adult, ie., the ability to think, that greatly influence its availability and effectiveness. For example, a Parent rule, learned in a healthy family, that says "You should think for yourself," will have a different effect on the use of the Adult than rules from a dysfunctional family that say, "You shouldn't be such a Know-It-All," and "You should always respect Authority." When faced with such limiting rules, the Child may make a decision to restrict the use of the Adult — "I don't want to think about it!"

Healthy individuals have access to all Ego States in any situation. They can always report how they feel (Child), what they think they should do (Parent) and what is most likely to happen if they take various actions (Adult). In the Adult Child, who, under duress, made an early decision not to think, the Adult often seems to be disconnected, even blocked off from the decisions and feelings stored in the Child. Often the Adult Child appears unable to get access to the Adult Ego State at all, especially when he is under stress. It is important to recognize the fact that because a person does not use his Adult does not mean he doesn't have one or that it is defective. Using the Adult is a choice made or decided on by the Child.

Transactions

If an individual can be described as operating from a Parent, Adult or Child Ego State, then the same concepts can be used to describe how people interact with each other. The study of the many patterns of transactions between people is described in detail in the basic literature of Transactional Analysis. In working with Co-dependent relationships, we are most concerned with certain characteristic patterns. Recognizing these patterns in moment-to-moment interactions helps the therapist to identify where specific interventions may be used.

An Adult Child tends to alternate between feeling and thinking, between Child and Adult. He operates as if there is a barrier, with the Child on one side and the Parent and Adult on the other. When he is on the Adult and Parent side of the barrier, he can function logically and competently, especially when thinking about what someone else is doing, needing or feeling. When he is on the Child side of the barrier, he may feel frightened, helpless, upset and needy.

In neither position is the Adult Child a fully functioning person. When he is on the Parent/Adult side of the barrier, he tries to operate without regard to his own needs and feelings. When he is on the Child side, he tends to operate as if *only* his feelings and needs are relevant, and doesn't have access to any problem-solving, reality-testing, negotiating or nurturing abilities. When he is in this Child position, he must depend on someone else to think for him and to manage the world for him.

Symbiosis

When the Adult Child leaves out one or more Ego States, operating as if he were somehow incomplete, he transacts with others in a characteristic way. He invites others to fill in what he is missing. He forms a relationship with another person who he perceives as having what he is missing. Unfortunately, the other person is often another Adult Child who also operates in an incomplete way.

The pattern of transactions that develops is called a "symbiosis". In this pattern, the transactions take place between the Parent or Adult of one person and the Child of the other. Within the symbiosis, they transact with each other as if there were only one whole person between the two of them: one contributes the Parent and Adult, while the other contributes the Child.

When *Jack* drinks, he is usually only in his Child, and Marci uses her Adult and Parent to take care of him. She makes excuses for him and generally enables him to continue his disease process by solving the problems *he* creates by his drinking.

Each partner typically operates from only one side of the barrier at a time, although they may occasionally switch sides with each other.

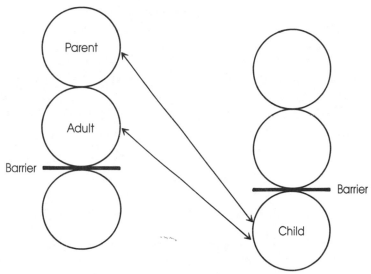

Figure 4.2. Symbiosis

When *Jack* is not in his Child, he is on the Parent/Adult side of the barrier, with his attention focused on what Marci does that is imperfect. He rationally and logically begins to point out all her mistakes, and then ends up yelling at and criticizing her. She cowers (becomes the helpless child she was when her father yelled at her), and using her Child, scurries to please him.

The partners may be symbiotic about some issues, eg., money, but not others, eg., food. A person may be typically in the Parent/ Adult position on one issue and in the Child position about something else. When the relationship is generally symbiotic, both partners will tend to stay on their "favorite" side of the barrier.

On occasion, they will both try to be on the same side of the barrier at the same time, but this is usually a brief competition for the favored position. They each try to take the same position

(Parent or Child) as the other, forcing the other to abandon his/
her position. After a few transactions like this, one of them usually
"wins". The "loser" of the contest has to give up the position he/
she is trying for and move back into the complementary position
in the symbiosis, eg.,

> **Marci** [Child]: *I'm so tired!*
> **Jack** [Child]: *I had a harder day than you did!*
> **Marci** [Giving up on Child and switching to Parent]: *I'll turn on the TV for you.*
>
> or
>
> **Marci** [Parent]: *You should spend more time with the children!*
> **Jack** [Parent]: *If you were any kind of a good mother, they wouldn't be so upset!*
> **Marci** [Parent]: *They need a father!*
> **Jack** [Giving up on Parent and switching to Child]: *Oh, all right, I'll try to do what you want.*

Symbiosis And Co-dependence

Understanding the dynamics of the symbiosis is the key to
working effectively with Co-dependence, because the attempt to
establish or maintain a symbiosis is the motivation for all Co-
dependent behavior.

Human beings need to be symbiotic in order to survive. An
infant only has a Child Ego State; the Parent and Adult are not yet
developed. The infant is therefore totally dependent on someone
else's problem-solving Adult and nurturing Parent to get his needs
met. In infancy, a healthy symbiotic transaction occurs when the
child expresses his needs directly, eg., crying when he is hungry,
and the parent responds to this demand for nurturing by (Adult)
thinking about what the baby needs and (Parent) taking care of
the needs.

If the infant's strong symbiotic needs for attachment are taken
care of appropriately, the natural process of development leads
him to the point where he is ready to break the symbiosis and
establish his autonomy. Although the need for attachment does
not disappear, it is now superceded by the equally strong need for
individuation. Healthy parenting through these critical stages
make it possible for the person to learn to balance his natural

needs for closeness and autonomy. (See Kaplan, *Oneness and Separateness: The Psychological Birth of the Human Infant*, for a beautiful description of this critical process.)

As we detail in later chapters, this process is rarely handled perfectly, even in the healthiest family. As a result, the Child is driven, by his own unmet developmental needs, to search for the kind of response from others (parenting) that will allow him to resolve these archaic developmental problems. In the process of trying to get these responses, he repeatedly attempts to create relationships in which he can establish, maintain and/or break symbiotic ties. This becomes a significant underlying motive in all the Adult Child's relationships.

Unfortunately, Adult Children tend to choose others who are just as incapable of providing the parenting they need as their own parents were. **Life becomes a never-ending search for the parent who will provide the nurturing for the lost Inner Child and allow it to finally grow up.**

Co-dependent behavior, ie., attempts to establish or maintain a symbiosis, can be observed in individual transactions, as well as in the patterns of transactions that occur over time. Whenever a person transacts from one side of the barrier between Adult and Child, and invites another to take the reciprocal position, then Co-dependent behavior is being observed. Any single Co-dependent transaction can be recognized and changed at any time. When the Co-dependent transactions are examined, the underlying reasons for the patterns often begin to emerge, eg.,

> **Therapist:** *Jack, what did you want to happen when you told Marci she wasn't a good mother?*
> **Jack:** *I wanted her to stop attacking me for being a bad father.*
> **T:** *That's what you wanted her to* **stop** *doing. What did you want her to do?*
> **J:** *I don't know . . . maybe for her to tell me she knows how hard I try.*
> **T:** *How did you let her know you wanted that from her?*
> **J:** *I guess I never did; I just attacked her.*
> **T:** *Have you ever wanted that kind of response from anyone else?*
> **J** (Angrily): *My mother never noticed how I took care of everyone in the family after my father left. She just complained when I didn't do it perfectly.*

T: *How old were you then?*
J: *Seven.*
T: *What did you want your mother to do?*
J: *Hug me once in a while and take care of me, too.*
T: *How did you let* her *know you wanted that?*
J: *I didn't; it wouldn't have done any good.*

By careful questioning, Jack learns that he is attacking Marci because his Inner Child wants her to love and care for him the way his Co-dependent mother never could. However, treating Marci as if she were his mother and not telling her what he needs from her, ensures that she will respond to him in a way that justifies his angry feelings. Jack recognizes now that his anger toward Marci originated with his anger at his mother, and he begins to work on releasing that anger in his therapy.

When Co-dependent behaviors are consistently examined, the Adult Child can learn to change them by paying attention and making new choices. However, the feelings that drive the Co-dependent behaviors are still in place, because the needs of the Inner Child for the missing appropriate parenting remain. The Adult Child must learn new, conscious ways of handling those needs. Methods for responding directly to these needs in the therapy sessions will be discussed in the "Treatment Implications" sections of each chapter on developmental stages.

Substitute Behavior

All people have needs and feelings that occur over and over again from birth until death. In a healthy situation, people do something to express these needs/feelings, and the environment (parents, spouse, friends, teachers, etc.) responds in some way that satisfies the need.

Jane and Edward decide to separate. Their six-year-old son, **Bryan,** is devastated. He cries and becomes hostile to Jane. Both parents assure him that they both still love him and will continue to take care of him. They set up a joint custody arrangement that works, and they continue to be responsive to his feelings.

In a dysfunctional situation, when the child expresses his needs, the environment doesn't respond appropriately.

When **Jack's** parents separated, he cried a lot, too. His father told him, "Shut up or I'll give you something to cry about!" His

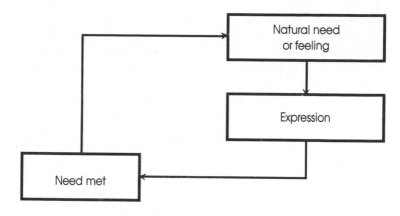

Figure 4.3. Need-Response Cycle: Healthy Cycle

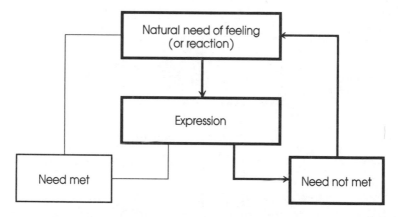

Figure 4.4. Need-Response Cycle: Dysfunctional Pattern

mother didn't say anything; she just stayed in her room for days at a time.

Bryan learned if he cried when he was upset, he could get nurtured. Jack learned that crying (expressing feelings) was useless or even dangerous. Bryan felt sad, but okay. Jack felt scared and helpless, and decided that he had better find something else to do when he had feelings.

Jack soon discovered that he could help his mother take care of the other kids; she seemed to feel better when he did, and came

out of the bedroom once in a while. He developed a substitute
behavior, taking care of others, but the original feelings of loss,
sadness, hurt and fear were never responded to or resolved. His
helpful, caretaking behavior was a substitute for making direct
demands on his Co-dependent mother to take care of him. At least
his caretaking behavior allowed him to find a place in his family.

As an adult, Jack tried to take care of his family by ignoring his
own needs and focusing on theirs, just as he learned to do when
he was a child. He didn't express his own feelings or receive much
affection. Even though he felt bad, his Parent kept telling him that
his feelings didn't count and that he should just keep on taking
care of everyone else.

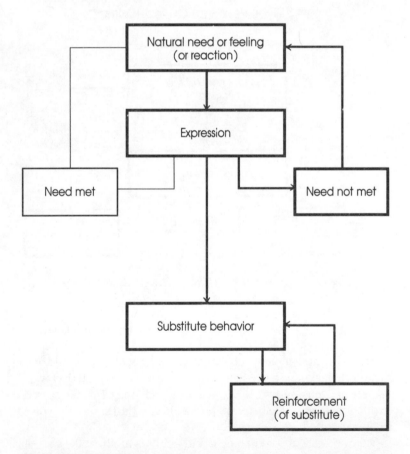

Figure 4.5. Need-Response Cycle: Creation of Substitute Behavior

In an attempt to medicate the pain of receiving no affection, either as a child or in his current life, Jack compounded his problems by turning to alcohol. Now, after two years of sobriety, he is learning to recognize the feelings of loss that he has carried since childhood. These feelings were buried and stored in his Inner Child, and shaped his relationship with Marci. He is beginning to learn how to pay direct attention to the unmet archaic needs and to use his problem-solving ability to do something direct about them.

Substitute behaviors are developed by children living in unresponsive, dysfunctional, often hostile, environments, in an attempt to get whatever caretaking and attention is available to them. Because these behaviors work to provide at least some attention, the Adult Child keeps using them.

Even though the Adult Child may sometimes experience his substitute behavior as "successful", ie., it appears to work to get some needs met, the substitute behaviors are fundamentally unhealthy. They do not fit into the Healthy Model. **Substitute behaviors always represent a denial of what the Inner Child really needs.** Furthermore, because the Adult Child is not expressing his real needs, he does not have any accurate information about how others would actually respond to those needs if he did express them. He is therefore missing the information about others' feelings and about the reality of his situation, and is not taking any initiative to get the information.

If the Adult Child does get his needs met in response to his substitute behavior, it will be because someone else has figured out what he needs and has given it to him. When this happens, it tends to reinforce the barrier between his Adult and Child, because he experiences that he can get some needs met without having to think about them. It is important to the Adult Child to keep the barrier strong, because, without it, he would begin to be in touch with the painful Child feelings associated with the unmet needs. This pain is buried, along with the awareness of the original needs; and the substitute behaviors, which cover both the original needs and feelings, seem to be all that is left.

When the patterns are examined, we can see that the original needs of the Inner Child were quite normal. If we can help the Inner Child learn to get directly what he has always needed, he can give up the unhealthy substitute behaviors.

When Co-dependent behavior is seen as a substitute for appropriate expressions of the Inner Child's needs, wants and feelings, the therapist's job becomes clear. The task is to recognize the substitute behavior for what it is and to help the client identify the specific original need that led to the creation of the substitute. Once this need has been identified, the therapist and client can problem-solve together, looking for ways the client can have the experience of having the original need met. This process is described in detail in the following chapters.

CHAPTER 5

A SYSTEMATIC TREATMENT APPROACH — PART 2, APPLICATIONS

Clients rarely present themselves as Co-dependents or as Adult Children of Alcoholics; they present problems they are trying to solve. Jack and Marci are each trying to change and control the other, while Nikki wants relief from her psychosomatic stomach disorder. Cory, a recovering alcoholic, wants to stop her compulsive overeating. Curt suppresses his emotions to keep from feeling anything uncomfortable, but can't get close to anyone as a result.

These and other Co-dependent behaviors can be understood as substitute behaviors, originally created by the Child in an attempt to meet some basic developmental need. As we discussed in Chapter 4, the therapist's job is to recognize substitute behavior for what it is, and to figure out which substitute behavior is hiding which natural, appropriate need of the Inner Child.

Viewed from this perspective, these behaviors can be seen as the Inner Child's cry for help: "I'm doing this because nothing else works — won't somebody please notice and give me what I really need!"

The therapist must help each client learn that **the presenting problem is a learned substitute behavior that the Inner Child is using in a creative attempt to meet some valid, important need.** Only then can the client get involved in decoding the substitute behavior. In this process, it is often important to get the client to shift his attention from the *content* of his problem to the *process* he uses to identify his own needs and to get them met. For example,

1. **Content:** "I feel inadequate at work."
2. **Process:** "I try to get reassurance that I'm okay by making helpful suggestions to people, but they reject and ignore me."

This client's "helpful" substitute behavior is not actually designed to be helpful to others; it is meant to *get* something for himself, without recognizing that his own Child's needs are motivating his behavior. As he learns to recognize that he tries to help others when he is wanting something for himself, he becomes more able to do something direct and effective about his own needs, eg.,

1. **Content:** "People don't pay any attention to me."
2. **Process:** (The client is speaking so softly that he can barely be heard across the desk.)

This client is not recognizing that his behavior has a direct impact on the results he experiences. As the behavior is pointed out, we can begin to examine how and why he is ineffective in getting the attention he needs.

There are a variety of techniques that can be used to help the client find a different way of thinking about the presenting problem. We usually begin by simply asking a series of questions:

1. "What do you want to change?"
2. "What keeps you from making that change?"
3. "What help, protection or resources do you need in order to make the change?"

4. "What do you need?"
5. "What are you doing to get that need met?"

Ego State Patterns

As a client tells his story, the therapist has the opportunity to observe an enormous amount of information about the client. There are features about his body position, word choice, sentence structure, facial expression, voice tone, response time and emotional tone. There are details about the content of the client's responses, such as his thoughts, feelings, actions, history, etc. There also is information about the therapist's internal response to the client, eg., attraction, repulsion, puzzlement, anger, sympathy, judgment, boredom, confusion, etc.

There are many ways for the therapist to sort all this information into usable patterns. The first pattern we look for is to determine what Ego State(s) the client is using. Recognizing Ego States enables us to notice when clients are inviting us to participate in symbiotic or Co-dependent transactions with them.

Characteristics of Ego States include:

1. **Child** — compliant, defiant, trying to please, trying to look good, inviting nurturing or sympathy, emotional
2. **Adult** — cool, detached, logical, organized
3. **Parent** — prejudiced, opinionated, judgmental, controlling, nurturing, over-solicitous

We also notice which Ego States we, as therapists, feel an urge to use in response to the client. Do we feel like nurturing the client or telling him to stop a particular behavior (Parent)? Do we feel intimidated, as if the client is judging us? Do we feel impelled to strive for the client's approval (Child)? When we pay attention to this information, we can calibrate our own internal responses and notice how our own reactions give us information about the client's patterns of interacting with others.

Marjie calmly and rationally describes how she meets her husband's unusual and offensive (to her) sexual demands. She readily admits that she perceives him as a little boy and herself as the mother who cares for him. When I ask how she feels about this situation, she tells me how *he* feels when she doesn't take care of

him. She also comments approvingly (and irrelevantly) about the
dress I'm wearing.

In our conversation, she is using her Adult and Parent, and her
description of the interaction with her husband sounds as if she only
uses her Adult and Parent with him. She does not acknowledge her
Child, even when she is invited to do so. I now suspect that she has
a serious problem either recognizing, acknowledging or sharing her
feelings, and that using her Adult and "staying cool" is probably a
substitute behavior.

In this case, Marjie is taking the Parent/Adult side of the symbiosis
with her husband. As she talks, my internal reaction is Child anger
at her husband; I suspect that is the feeling she would have, if she
were to allow herself to feel. This observation then leads me to ask
about her childhood experiences with anger, which, in turn, lead to
significant information about the sexual abuse she suffered in her
dysfunctional family.

Gina, on the other hand, appears so nervous she can hardly talk.
She stares at her hands and twists her handkerchief in response to
my questions. She occasionally glances at me, but still doesn't
answer the questions. She is clearly in her Child.

If I were to act according to what I feel in response to her
behavior, I would suggest answers to the questions for her and
would try to make her feel more comfortable. I would use my Adult
to think for her and my Parent to take care of her; I would be
accepting her invitation to join her in a symbiosis.

Because I know that she holds a responsible job, I am sure that
she is not really as helpless as she is presenting herself to be. I
suspect that her helplessness is a substitute behavior, covering a
genuine Inner Child need for nurturing. I test my theory by acting
helpless myself, whining at her that I don't know what to do. (I
respond to her invitation to be symbiotic by giving her a Child
response, rather than the Parent/Adult response she is trying to get.)
She indignantly tells me with her Parent that I'm the therapist and
I'm supposed to be helping her. I resume using my Adult and
suggest that this is a job we can only do with her cooperation. The
symbiotic pattern is broken, for the moment, and she starts to
answer my questions.

The Passivity Syndrome: Discounting

Another important way to sort the variety of information
presented by the client is to look for evidence of passive behavior

and passive thinking. "Passive" in this sense refers to any kind of thinking or acting that is a substitute for taking initiative to respond to the needs of the Inner Child.

Recognizing and confronting passive behavior and/or passive thinking ("discounting") is a critical step in helping clients learn to create (or re-create) the healthy cycle of feeling a need, doing something direct and effective about it and getting an appropriate response. Passive behaviors (described below) can be directly observed; discounting is a thinking process that cannot be directly observed, but can be inferred from what the client reveals about the way he is thinking.

In *The Cathexis Reader*, Jacqui Lee Schiff, et al describe four levels of discounting.

Discounting The Problem

- A mother whose children were removed from the home because of repeated abuse says, "What problem? There's no problem in this family; we're a model family."
- After a second DUI arrest, a man says, "I don't have any drinking problem."
- The family walks around Daddy, who is passed out on the living room floor, and nobody makes any comment.
- An Adult Child who repeatedly witnessed abuse of his siblings says, "I had a normal childhood."

This is denial in its purest form. A person who is discounting at this level is thinking in a way that omits any information about his own feelings, anyone else's feelings and especially about the reality of the situation. As a result, he behaves as if there *is* no problem.

Discounting The Significance Of The Problem

- "My mother only threatened suicide once in a while — I managed okay."
- A woman who becomes abusive after two drinks says, "I never drink before 5:00 p.m."
- A pregnant woman who works full-time on swing shift and is responsible for three preschoolers during the day says, "I'm just tired."
- "Everyone in our family was nervous: that's just the way we are."

In this form of discounting, the person is aware that there is a problem, but minimizes it by not thinking about the impact of it, and by taking the position that there is no reason for it, that it's "just the way it is". Again, if there is no reason for the problem, the person can justify, in her own thinking, that she can't be expected to take any initiative to solve it.

Discounting The Solvability Of The Problem

- "I couldn't manage without him," spoken by a woman whose husband hasn't worked in two years.
- "If I have to tell you what I want, it means you don't really love me."
- "Nobody could satisfy that bitch."

These examples typify a process of distorting information, often through exaggeration. The basic thinking is that there really is a problem, it does have an impact and there are reasons for it. However, because *nothing* can be done about it, you surely can't expect me to do anything about it.

Discounting The Capabilities Or Feelings Of The Person (Self Or Other)

- "I just can't make her listen!"
- "If she really knew me, she wouldn't like me."
- "I'm not scared (angry, sad, etc.)."
- "I don't care!"
- "I'm no good."
- "I'm so stupid!"
- "I can't stand it!"

Discounting the self or other is usually some form of defining oneself as "special" or different from others, such as "Someone else could handle this, but *I* can't do it, because I'm too nervous, too young, too old, too insecure, too busy, etc." In general, **people discount when they are unwilling, for whatever reason, to take the responsibility to do what they think they would have to do if they were not discounting.** Therefore, discounting becomes the internal justification for not taking action to do something about a problem or about an Inner Child need or feeling.

The Passivity Syndrome: Passive Behavior

The observable behavior that is produced by discounting can be seen as passive. Passive behaviors are designed to establish or maintain symbiotic transactions with others. When a person behaves passively, he covertly invites someone else to take responsbility for his problem. According to Schiff, the passive behaviors are:

Doing Nothing (about the problem)

- *Bob* has a bad cough, but continues to smoke. He says, "I'm just nervous and, besides, everyone coughs sometimes."
- *Sam* is depressed, because he is not getting enough strokes from other people. He deals with it by sitting at home, alone, whenever he isn't working at his solitary job.
- *Martha's* 15-year-old son comes home drunk several times a week. She worries, but says and does nothing.

In one case, the person who is doing nothing passively creates a situation in which any problem-solving that takes place will have to be initiated by someone else. If the person transacts with others about the problem, they usually invite the other person into a symbiotic pattern.

Overadaptation

This means that the person is doing what he thinks he is supposed to do, without really thinking about it, such as

- Reluctantly listening to several hours of complaining over the telephone
- Engaging in sexual activity because you are expected to
- Staying in an abusive relationship
- Making excuses for or covering up for a chemically dependent person

When a person is behaving in an overadapted fashion, he is usually discounting himself. If asked why he is doing something, he will be unable to answer the question in terms of *his own* needs, feelings and goals.

Often, the person who is overadapting to the needs and feelings of other people is doing so without any direct information about what the others really want. He is operating on what he *thinks* they want or on what somebody in his past may have wanted. It would usually not occur to him to ask if his assumptions are correct in the current situation.

Surprisingly, rebellious behavior can also be understood as a form of overadaptation. The person who is being rebellious, like the person who is being compliant, is not identifying what *he* wants. He is reacting to what *someone else* wants by being oppositional about it.

Overadaptation may be using the Parent and Adult to take care of someone else's Child or acting like a helpless Child and inviting someone else to be the Parent; it depends on what role an individual learned to assume in the family system. In either case, playing the role involves doing what is expected.

Agitation

Agitation involves engaging in repetitive, often compulsive activity, which temporarily draws attention away from a problem. Examples of compulsive activity include:

- Overeating, drinking, smoking, working, spending, gambling, exercising, using drugs, etc.
- Tearing a tissue to shreds
- Twisting a handkerchief
- Fiddling with a cup
- Drumming fingers

When a person is agitating, he is draining energy away from the discomfort that would lead him to pay attention to the existence of a problem. Agitation is frequently a signal that the person is working to suppress some strong emotion. Agitation usually involves an attempt to stay out of touch with the feelings of the Inner Child.

Incapacitation Of Self Or Violence Toward Self Or Others

- Losing control or consciousness through abuse of chemicals
- Becoming ill from overwork
- Going to bed with a migraine headache
- Destroying property — anything from burning a hole in a chair to totalling a car

When a person is incapacitiated or violent, he essentially wins the Child position in the symbiosis. His behavior forces someone else — often someone in authority — to take over the Parent and Adult position.

All of these passive behaviors are substitute behaviors; they cover some unmet Inner Child needs and feelings, and they are used instead of doing something effective to satisfy those needs. They are like the visible tip of an iceberg; they signal that there is something else hidden beneath what is obvious.

Passivity Confrontation

When passive behaviors are confronted and explored, the Co-dependent thinking and the reasons for the discounting become apparent. These reasons usually can be traced to ineffective parenting and incomplete development of skills necessary for effective adult functioning.

Calling the client's attention to discounting and/or passive behavior helps the client become aware of problems in current situations, as well as unresolved problems that occurred earlier in a client's lifetime. When a client moves past the denial and truly acknowledges a problem, strong feelings, often grief and/or rage, are experienced, and healing begins. Once these problems are identified, a treatment plan can be developed.

The purpose of confronting the client's substitute behavior is to identify the need underlying it, in order to establish a healthy pattern of recognizing needs and taking appropriate action to get those needs met. Expanding the "Need/Response Diagram" from Chapter 4 provides some guidelines for making these interventions. (See Figure 5.1.)

Identifying the Need

The simplest confrontation of substitute behavior is to ask the person what he is really needing or feeling when he:

- Reaches for a cigarette
- Insults someone he loves
- Doesn't answer a question
- Tells a lie
- Fills his life with work
- Withdraws behind a wall

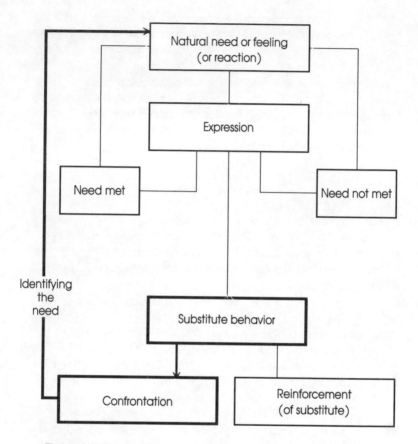

Figure 5.1. Confrontation of Substitute Behavior: Identifying the Need

Some recovering Adult Children become adept at answering. They pause and pay attention to the signals that come from within, and the answers come:

- "I need to cry about what I've lost."
- "I need a hug."
- "I need to rest."
- "I need to tell someone I'm angry."
- "I need to know I'm wanted."
- "I need to be held."

Once a need is known, it can be expressed to someone who can respond. When the need is responded to, the healthy cycle is complete, and the need for the substitute behavior gradually diminishes.

Unfortunately, Co-dependents in the early stages of recovery usually can't answer this question immediately. For someone who grew up in an environment in which her needs and feelings were discounted, identifying her Inner Child needs takes training, practice, permission and experience. A safe environment is required, where the Inner Child can be recognized and responded to in a healthy way (see Chapter 7, "Treatment Environment").

Behavioral Interventions

The therapist can help the client discover the underlying need by asking leading questions, as we illustrated in Chapter 4 with Jack. When we discovered that Jack's Inner Child was seven, we used the developmental road map (see Chapter 16, "The Latency Stage") to supplement his description of what his Inner Child needed. Seven-year-olds need to get acknowledgment and recognition from parents and others when they are active in doing things and solving problems.

Once the original need is identified, either by the client or by the therapist, we can intervene by prescribing a behavior for the client to do that is a natural expression of the need or feeling. When the client engages in the behavior, we can either provide an appropriate response in the treatment environment or carefully instruct the client to practice the new behavior in another safe environment where he is likely to receive an appropriate response. This behavioral practice often helps the client to become aware of the original need, and reestablishes the healthy cycle. (See Figure 5.2.)

We made a behavioral intervention with Jack, suggesting that he talk to us about things he was attempting to do, and let us stroke his Inner Child for doing those things. When Jack "acted as if" he were expressing the normal needs of his seven-year-old Child, and we responded to him, the buried sadness, fear and anger began to emerge. We helped Jack express those old feelings (see Chapters 8 and 12, "Working With Feelings", Parts 1 and 2), and he eventually was able to grieve for the nurturing he had not gotten when he was seven.

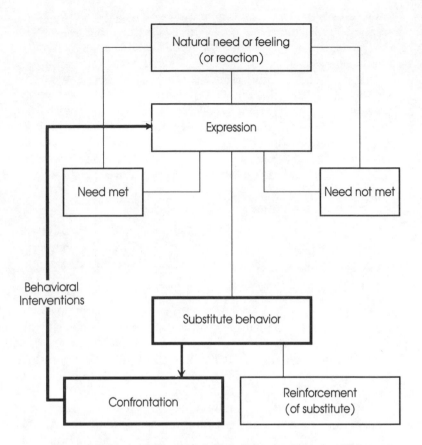

Figure 5.2. Confrontation of Substitute Behavior: Behavioral Interventions

Jack decided to tell Marci about what he was attempting to do for the family. A dialogue ensued, in which she could give him feedback about which of the things he was doing worked and which ones didn't. He learned to notice his own feelings during these conversations, breaking down the barrier between Adult and Child. When he became aware of his feelings, he asked Marci about hers, helping her break down her own barrier. He could then suggest activities that would be beneficial to both of them. One area of Co-dependent behavior began to recede.

Behavioral intervention, asking the client to behave as if he is expressing a need or feeling we suspect he has, is a powerful tool. It enables the client to reestablish a healthy cycle of feeling a need, expressing it appropriately and arranging for a healthy response. When used in the protected setting of the therapy group, it can help the Adult Child learn that there is not necessarily something wrong with him if he doesn't get the response he wants.

Meeting Needs Directly

Another possible intervention strategy is for the therapist to guess what the original need was and meet the need, without having the client ask to have the need met. Sometimes this is appropriate when a client is badly upset.

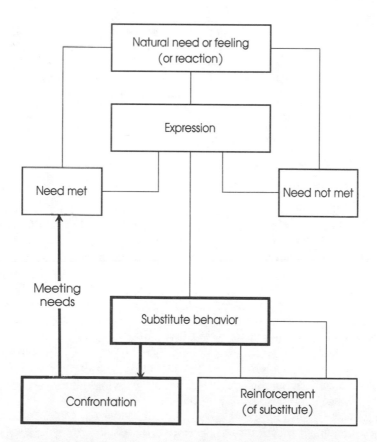

Figure 5.3. Confrontation of Substitute Behavior: Meeting Needs

Magda came into my office upset and almost incoherent, because her Co-dependent partner in an addictive relationship was leaving. I observed that she was operating mostly from an infant Child Ego State. I offered to hold her, and she accepted. I treated her as if she were an infant for about thirty minutes. Then I asked her to sit up, and I explained that I had been responding to her Inner Child who was so upset, and that in the future, if she felt that way, she could know that her Child needed to be held and could use her Adult to ask for it. She left relaxed and making plans to spend time with supportive friends until the severest pain of abandonment passed.

If I hadn't given her the information about asking next time, I would have run the risk of establishing myself as the all-knowing parent with whom she can relax into another dependent symbiotic relationship. Meeting the Inner Child's needs directly is a useful intervention to calm an extremely upset client. However, it is also a dangerous intervention, because it can reinforce the barrier between Adult and Child, instead of helping to break it down. Most intervention should be aimed at helping the clients think about their own feelings and about what they need to do to resolve them (see Chapter 8).

Prescribing Another Substitute

Another confrontation of substitute behavior is to suggest another less destructive substitute until the Adult Child is ready to address the needs of the Inner Child. Having a client stop overeating and attend Overeaters Anonymous instead is a very useful confrontation of a substitute behavior. Doing the Twelve-Step Program helps stabilize the client. When the abstinence from the addictive behavior is well-established, work on healing the Inner Child can begin. (Sometimes, however, clients will only give up their addictions when the Inner Child begins to receive direct nurturing.)

Sometimes a client is reluctant to accept confrontation, however gentle it may be. Confrontation literally means "to face". For some clients, really facing their problems means allowing themselves to experience some very painful realities: they have been living a lie, they have been hurt, their parents let them down, others will see how imperfect they are and therefore abandon them, they must reorganize their lives and they must change.

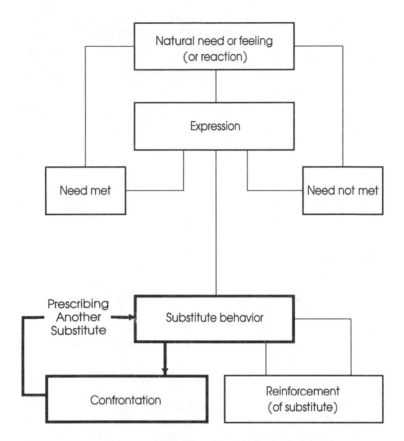

Figure 5.4. Confrontation of Substitute Behavior:
Prescribing Another Substitute

All of these recognitions may be painful and/or terrifying to a client, who may work hard to avoid the pain. He may block his awareness, not respond to what is said to him and switch rapidly from one form of passive behavior to another.

There are some simple but powerful techniques to help a client through these blocks. When a client doesn't answer a question:

- Ask the same question again, using exactly the same words and tone of voice.
- Ask the client if he is aware that he didn't answer the question; once that discussion is complete, ask the original question again.

- If the client changes the subject, say, "First answer my question, then we can talk about the new subject."
- If the client answers only part of the question, ask him to complete the answer.
- If the client responds with a long story, interrupt after a while and ask, "How is this an answer to the question?" You may have to ask the client if he remembers what the question is; if he doesn't, repeat it.
- If the client cries, shouts, faints or escalates some other inappropriate behavior, deal with that behavior, and then decide whether to keep asking the original question.
- Ask the client to take responsibility for refusing to answer: ask him to say out loud, "I won't tell you the answer to your question."

Another useful technique is to ask the client to fill in the blanks in the "Think Structure", adapted from Pam Levin's book, *Becoming The Way We Are*. (See Figure 5.1.)

Cory completed the Think Structure as follows: "I feel scared because I think that if I get close to a man I will be sexually abused, instead of talked to and listened to, and so I binge eat. I need to get close slowly and keep checking on whether the man I'm with both talks and listens to me."

Experienced clients can use this technique to decode most substitute behavior and figure out the response they need. The therapist can lead less experienced clients through the process.

The way the client answers these questions will show the missing or impaired abilities that can be traced to unmet developmental needs. Sharing this information with the client leads to discovering why these skills haven't been learned. This process frequently evokes suppressed childhood memories and emotions. The clients gradually begin to understand how learning to recognize and care for the Inner Child will help them solve the presenting problems.

The resulting treatment plan, agreed to by the therapist and the client, must be both logical and emotionally satisfying to the client. The logical part explains the connection between unmet developmental needs and current problems; the emotional part touches the Inner Child, offering an opportunity to grow in a protected and nurturing environment.

Chart 5.1. Think Structure

I feel _____ ,
    (emotion: sad, mad, scared, etc.)

because I think
that if I _____ ,
    (behave in a specific way, eg., ask for what I want, tell
    what really happened, get angry, etc.)

I will be _____ ,
    (treated in some specific negative way, eg., hit, laughed
    at, ignored, abandoned, etc.)

instead of _____ ,
    (treated how I want to be treated in response to the
    above behavior, eg., listened to, loved, hugged, talked
    to, have appropriate limits set, given what I want, etc.)

and so I _____ .
    (substitute behavior I engage in: drink, stay in addictive
    relationship, hide, *act* scared or angry or sad, don't show
    feelings, etc.)

In order to solve this
problem, I need to _____ ,
    (do the specific behavior I identified above)

and have someone _____ .
    (give me the specific response I identified
    above)

I will ask _____ to help me, and I will do it
    (person)

by _____ .
  (date)

As the healthy cycle is reestablished, the pain from the past arises and must be experienced and released. Then the Adult Child learns to know himself, his own needs and wants, and learns to think about creating situations where those needs can be responded to. As this process continues, the Inner Child is embraced and becomes a useful, healthy part of the grown-up person.

CHAPTER 6

GOALS OF TREATMENT

Two years after the scene in Chapter 1, and six months after completing treatment, Jenny writes that she has spent several days with her father. She is pleased and surprised at her ability to communicate with him about who she has become, and is delighted by his accepting response. Her letter demonstrates that she is now functioning as a mature individual who is using her own resources to manage her relationships appropriately.

She has clearly overcome the pain and the defensive protection that she had used to keep the world at bay (her fantasy hero was a character in a novel, a "strong, silent type" man who when interfered with became extremely violent). She now knows what she needs, including closeness with others, and acts appropriately to meet those needs.

She no longer fears losing her individuality in close relationships. She is no longer angry at the world for not meeting her expectations, and takes an active role in getting things to work the way she wants them to.

She demonstrates that she now has the tools she would have had if she had grown up in a normal environment, tools for solving the normal problems of living and relating to others.

Jenny, like most Adult Children, came to therapy because she was in pain. She spent most of her time feeling angry, sad, scared or numb, and she functioned poorly in her work and in her personal relationships. Initially, when we asked her what she wanted to work on in her therapy, she said "Everything!"

The first task in an effective therapy process is for the client and therapist to mutually define the outcome to be achieved. The outcome should be stated in a way that makes sense to the client, and that she can own. At the same time, it must be put in terms that are reasonably concrete, specific and achievable; otherwise the therapist may be in the position of promising impossible results. It would be a mistake to accept Jenny's emotional statement that she wants to change "everything" as a valid treatment contract.

Even when clearly stated, a client's goals for therapy will probably be relatively long-range and global. Part of the therapist's job is to break the larger goals down into smaller, more specific ones, so that progress can be assessed more readily. Most clients will state goals in terms of feeling better or thinking differently. We have found that redefining these goals in behavioral terms makes them more specific and more observable, and provides many more opportunities to stroke the client for progress.

If the therapist has a systematic model of human behavior and interaction, it can be useful in the process of defining goals. It is as if the client describes the landscape around her, from her point of view. The therapist who possesses a good map of the territory can recognize the client's probable location and can see, from that perspective, how she can get to safer and more livable ground. The therapist helps the client walk the path safely, avoiding quicksand and poison ivy.

In the previous chapter, we began to describe some of the ways of recognizing what is immediately in front of us, ie., the way a person is functioning at a given moment. This information is amplified in the next chapter. The most important features of the map, ie., the developmental theory, are shown in the chapters that describe the specific developmental stages of childhood. In the remainder of this chapter, we will show how the developmental model identifies the healthy behaviors and skills that can be used as specific therapeutic goals.

Therapist: *What do you want to change?*
Jenny: *Everything! Everything I do and feel and think is crummy!*
T: *It sounds like you are very critical of yourself.* (J agrees.) *How did you learn to do that?*
J: *That's how my parents treated me.*
T: *How did you feel about it when they were doing it?*
J: *Terrible, of course! They were really mean; he was drunk all the time, and I think she was really crazy. Everything they ever said to me was critical.*
T: *If you felt so bad when they treated you like that, why are you doing it to yourself?*
J: *I guess I didn't see that I was; it just seems normal. Besides, I don't think I know how to do anything else.*
T: *Well, part of the reason you feel so bad all the time is that you are treating yourself as badly as your parents treated you, and it's time for you to stop doing that. Even if you don't know what else to do, you can learn.* **We can teach you here how to treat yourself with more nurturing.** *Meanwhile, you can start to pay attention to what you are saying to yourself, so that* **you can learn not to be so critical of yourself.**

When Jenny started therapy, we observed that she had few of the living skills she needed — skills she could easily have learned if she had grown up in a healthy environment. Guided by the map of the characteristics of each stage of development, we helped Jenny set goals to learn the skills appropriate to each stage.

Fortunately, any skills that were not learned in childhood can be learned as an adult. The adult learning of skills that should have been learned in childhood is much easier when the person knows that a particular skill is missing, and that she is trying to learn it. Often Adult Children are unaware of what they lack; they only know that somehow other people can do things they are unable to do themselves.

Bonding Stage Skills

Healthy parenting in this first stage of development, from birth to approximately six to nine months, lays the foundation for learning to recognize physical needs and to initiate doing something to meet them. On a more psychological level, healthy development in this stage leads to having a basic sense of having an impact on the world. Healthy parents respond as best they can to the baby's demands. (See Chapter 10, "Bonding Stage", for a detailed discussion.)

In a dysfunctional family, the baby's needs may be ignored while parents struggle with their own difficulties. An Adult Child who suffered extreme abuse or neglect may no longer even notice the body signals that certain physical functions need attention.

Healthy adults, on the other hand, are able and willing to ask for what they need. A person who received adequate response to his developmental needs in this stage will be able to:

1. Notice physical needs and sensations without feeling extreme agitation about them
2. Feel physical sensations when he is hungry, and know that those sensations can be relieved with food
3. Eat when he is hungry, and be willing to skip a meal when he isn't hungry
4. Notice when he is thirsty and be willing to drink water or other fluids to relieve his thirst
5. Notice when he is too hot or too cold and be willing to dress to maintain comfort; he is also willing to see that heating or cooling controls be adjusted
6. Recognize physical signs of fatigue and be willing to take time for rest and renewal, even if only a brief stretch or break
7. Notice the need to urinate or defecate, and be willing to take time to do so, even if he needs to excuse himself during a meeting
8. Notice when his air is polluted and be willing to ask others not to smoke, or remove himself from noxious odors
9. Notice when he needs attention from other people, and do something to get it
10. Notice when he needs time away from other people and be willing to arrange to take it, even if only for a few minutes

The characteristic problems that can arise from inadequate parenting are described, stage by stage, in Chapter 9, "Diagnosing Developmental Dysfunctions".

Exploratory Stage Skills

Appropriate parenting for a child in this stage, from six to nine months to 18 to 24 months, allows the child to learn to identify what she wants and to go after it. (See Chapter 11, "Exploratory Stage" for a detailed discussion.) She learns that it is safe to take initiative to get what she wants.

In a dysfunctional family, the child learns to notice what pleases her parents. In order to avoid trouble and maintain a reasonable supply of strokes, she ends up being guided by the expectations and demands of others, rather than by her own internal desires.

As an adult, a person with healthy parenting from this stage will be able to:

1. Be comfortable, even positive about exploring new things

2. Enjoy learning about new places, by exploring an unfamiliar part of town, a new store or a new city

3. Be interested in tasting new foods

4. Take classes on unfamiliar subjects, just because they look interesting

5. Take appropriate safety precautions during her explorations, so she doesn't get hurt

6. Accept temporary discomfort, if it will lead to something better or more interesting

7. Stop doing something when she discovers she has had enough, or if she doesn't like it

Separation Stage Skills

The "Terrible Two's" stage, from 18 to 24 months to 30 to 36 months, is when the child learns the foundation for independence and autonomy. Children learn to separate from their parents and become independent during this stage by rebelling and learning appropriate limits. In dysfunctional families this rebellious behavior is either suppressed or not limited at all; sometimes it alternates between both extremes.

This is the stage in which people develop the ability and the willingness to think for themselves and to consider the wants and needs of others. They learn to recognize that their actions have consequences, and that they can choose what they want to do, based on those consequences. (See Chapter 13, "Separation Stage", for a detailed discussion.)

In Transactional Analysis terms, this is the stage in which the Child decides to use the Adult as a tool, to help him figure out how to get what he needs. When Adult and Child work together, the person can:

1. Know that he is as important as other people — not more important or less important
2. Say *no* out loud to things that he doesn't want to do
3. Maintain his individuality in relationships
4. Be comfortable knowing that he is different and separate from others
5. Actively oppose things he believes to be destructive to himself, others, or the environment.

Socialization Stage Skills

During preschool years (three to five), the child in a healthy family is busy learning an astonishing variety of social and psychological skills. As her language ability grows, she learns to ask questions. She learns how to get information about what she is doing and feeling, and about what others are doing and feeling. She learns to use her imagination, and can think and feel about the things that she imagines, as well as about the things that really happen. (See Chapter 14, "Socialization Stage", for a detailed discussion.)

Truthful dialogue with children is essential for healthy development in this stage. In dysfunctional families, this dialogue is missing, and children make up explanations for why their worlds are so chaotic.

Once a person has learned the fundamental ability to distinguish between thoughts, feelings and actions, she can:

1. Identify and talk about feelings, her own and others'
2. Understand that just thinking or feeling something cannot change anything in the physical world; that only doing something about thoughts or feelings causes reactions
3. Give up the belief in magic, and understand how far her power extends
4. Notice when feelings and behaviors are incongruent, eg., someone shouting, "I am not angry."

5. Attempt to have others clarify incongruent communications before responding to them, eg., "You sound angry, but you say you're not; what do you want?"
6. Feel grief when she cannot get what she wants or needs, and can use the grief to let go and release the energy

Latency Stage Skills

Between the ages of six and twelve years, healthy children think about doing tasks and activities. They argue with their parents about why they should or shouldn't do things or treat people or property in a particular way. In dysfunctional families, children are not permitted to argue. They may be told rigidly to do something in a particular way, or may just be expected to do it with no instruction whatever. They are not taught to think about what they are doing — just to do what is expected.

Adults who have experienced healthy parenting through this stage can:

1. Get help or information when they need to do something they don't know how to do, eg., take lessons, ask experts, etc.
2. Decide how well any task needs to be done, eg., what level of skill do I want to develop at tennis
3. Can finish most tasks they start
4. Can decide not to finish any given task, based on thinking about the consequences of finishing or not finishing, eg., they can abandon a half-finished project and decide to give or throw it away
5. Can understand and communicate the reasons for their beliefs and feelings
6. Can negotiate with others about differences, and reach solutions where everybody wins

Adolescent Skills

Adolescents in healthy families gradually separate psychologically and physically from their families. In dysfunctional families, adolescents are either abruptly separated from the family (run away or get kicked out), or remain enmeshed indefinitely (keeping the family secrets, always rescuing and being responsible for taking care of other family members, etc.).

Adults who have had a healthy adolescence can:
1. Live independently, negotiating with others to get what they need and want, including sex
2. Maintain a sense of themselves when participating in intimate relationships
3. Acknowledge their connection to others
4. Live *inter*dependently and still remain antonomous

Each of the skills learned at the various developmental stages becomes an important component of the person's ability to function within the Healthy Model (see Chapter 4). They help the person learn how to take initiative, to know what she needs, to find out and deal appropriately with what others need and to assess the reality of the situation around her. Only through the use of these basic skills can she manage the continuous process of getting what she wants and needs, in a world where others also have wants and needs.

When a client reports or demonstrates an inability to do any of these basic skills, we can use the information to target the specific developmental stage where the problem probably originated. Out of this information can come a proposal of a specific goal for the treatment process.

Treatment goals for our clients are based on assessing the areas in which they can function in healthy ways and on discovering the gaps in their learning. These gaps usually cluster around behaviors ordinarily learned at a specific stage (or stages) of child development.

Using the information from the developmental model, along with data from the client's history, we can estimate the approximate age of the Inner Child. We then create a treatment plan which will enable the Adult Child to learn the missing skills and beliefs. The specific elements of the treatment plans, and the behavioral prescriptions that are an essential part of each plan, are described in detail in the chapters on developmental stages.

CHAPTER 7

THE TREATMENT ENVIRONMENT

Accepting confrontation, giving up denial, dropping substitute behavior and learning new skills all require great courage. Most recovering Adult Children feel afraid, even terrified, when asked to experience and express the original, uncensored needs and feelings of their Inner Child. As they begin this process, they re-experience the internalized Parent rules of the dysfunctional family: "Don't Talk", "Don't Feel" and "Don't Trust" (Claudia Black, *It Will Never Happen To Me*). The very idea of breaking these old rules is terrifying for most Adult Children; they believe, from early experience, that the world will be unresponsive and/or punitive. Most Adult Children have an inner conviction that their survival depends on following the old rules.

These rules led the Inner Child to conclude that he was unlovable, inadequate, powerless, and that he was probably the cause of his family's problems. Therefore, these old rules need to be broken. The Inner Child wants and needs to trust, feel and talk, but is fearful of being hurt again.

Most Adult Children have spent a lifetime struggling with this dilemma. **The Inner Child of a Co-dependent person secretly searches for healthy parenting, testing everyone who is strong and/or nurturing to see if he will provide it.** They hope for the best, but expect to be hurt.

Relationships are established over and over again with others whom the Adult Child hopes will provide the longed-for parental response. These relationships seldom work, because they are usually with others from dysfunctional homes, who also fear talking, feeling or trusting. In these relationships, one of the partners typically gets scared, pulls back, betrays trust, tries to control, is betrayed, etc. (see Janet Woititz, *The Struggle for Intimacy*), proving once again that it was a good idea to follow the original family rules.

In therapy, where unmet needs from childhood are being identified, **the Inner Child looks hopefully and fearfully to the therapist, and asks, "Can I get what I need here?"** In corrective parenting, we strive to create an environment where those needs *can* be met. As Paine-Gernee (1986) puts it, "Needs that were never met in childhood come rushing forward into the therapeutic relationship. Working with this dependency is part of the healing, for what ACoA's often need is to be taken care of, to be the child they never were. Then in therapy they can truly grow up, developing a genuine maturity and a capacity for self-care."

Psychologically, the therapist *is* the client's parent, whether or not either of them consciously acknowledges that relationship. Corrective parenting is a strategy that deliberately uses this reality to create healing experiences for the Inner Child. To be effective in helping the Inner Child grow up, the parenting that takes place in therapy must be done in a way that supports and encourages the client's growth and autonomy, rather than done in a way that undercuts the client and feeds the therapist's need to manage his or her own Co-dependence issues.

Providing corrective parenting experiences for the lost and lonely Inner Child is a task that must be done with honesty and integrity, or else we risk repeating and reinforcing the negative experiences and decisions from the original dysfunctional family.

For the client to learn to nurture her own Inner Child, she must be able to incorporate specific permissions and instructions about dealing with her own needs and feelings. She needs to experience a healthy environment in which it is very clear that the original family rules do not apply.

In a healthy family, children learn to love themselves by being treated with love, respect and appropriate limits. For an Adult Child to learn to love and care for the Inner Child, the therapy sessions must create an environment similar to a healthy family: permission to function appropriately and effectively must be provided, along with instructions on how to do so. To create a safe and consistent environment for healing the Inner Child, the therapist must explicitly state these permissions, and frequently encourage, model and reinforce them.

Although most psychotherapy begins in individual sessions, we find that a group setting is more effective in helping clients to accept and test the new permissions. In a group setting that is modeled after a healthy family, the Adult Child has many opportunities to observe rules that differ from the dysfunctional family rules. Feelings and talking are encouraged. Information about building trust is provided gradually.

When the group structure is open-ended, new clients can observe more experienced clients following the new permissions. By observing how group members are actually treated when they break the dysfunctional family rules, the new group member can learn to risk and trust.

The permissions described below are general rules that can be presented in a variety of ways. The explanations and examples we present here are what we do in *our* groups. Use them as guidelines, rather than as absolutes.

We believe these permissions provide the necessary conditions for Adult Children to feel safe enough to remember old traumas, to grieve for the nurturing they didn't receive and to learn the skills they need to function in a healthy way. This learning can best take place in an atmosphere of love, respect and support. This atmosphere is created by conscientiously establishing and following these rules.

Rule Number One

It is okay to talk about your past and present problems, especially problems in your family; when you talk about problems, we will help you focus on thinking about how to solve them.

This permission is encouraged by having each client start every group with a statement about what he will work on in that session. Nobody gets to hide.

New clients, who may be uncomfortable, are encouraged to say so and to say what they want to do about it. They usually ask to observe, and we encourage them to ask questions about things they don't understand. Throughout the group we are alert to nonverbal signals that indicate that the new client is having some reaction to the situation. If the client does not take initiative to report on his reaction, we ask.

When clients describe a problem in their current life, we usually ask, "What do you want to happen?" and "Do you think it is possible to achieve that outcome?" If yes, "What do you need to do to achieve it?" If no, "What do you think is possible to achieve?" and "How?".

Talking about current and past problems is modeled by more experienced group members. In addition, we use many stories and examples from our own lives, from the media and from our therapeutic experience to illustrate the ways in which problems can actually be solved. We try to concentrate on examples that show the use of the healthy model, ie., taking into account one's own feelings, those of the other person and the reality of the situation.

Rule Number Two

Talking about feelings is appropriate, and allowing yourself to actually feel them and express them directly is even better.
Permission to express feelings is stated in a variety of ways.

1. "It's normal to mourn, even when you are giving up something that isn't good for you."
2. "All of your feelings are okay", eg., when a client thinks he shouldn't feel sad about leaving a destructive relationship.
3. "What are you feeling?" (This is asked when it looks like a client is feeling something and trying not to be noticed.)
4. "It's okay to cry."

Clients are often reluctant to express feelings, because they fear that those feelings will be ignored or ridiculed. Whenever feelings are expressed, we acknowledge the client positively for expressing the feelings and ask what other response they need. (See Chapter 8, "Working With Feelings," for more detail.)

Rule Number Three

Communicate directly with others present; talk *to* people, rather than *about* them.

Often a client will ask the therapist a question about someone else in the group. We usually ask the client to direct that question to the person they are curious about, and we stay alert to the possible need to help the second client answer honestly and respectfully. Sometimes a question is asked about a client who is acting as if he is a small child, or who is deeply engrossed in some intense emotional work. At those times, we answer the question ourselves, and encourage the questioner to ask it again when the second client is in a better position to answer it.

Rule Number Four

When you are expressing your feelings, say how you are *feeling* about the other person's *behavior*.

When a client has feelings or reactions to another client, we encourage him to express it directly to the other person. At the same time, we are teaching and modeling *how to* express feelings in a way that can be useful. In this way, clients can apply what they learn about how to communicate in their interactions with others outside of the therapy sessions, such as saying:

1. "I'm angry at you for doing that," rather than "You're a jerk!"
2. "I feel scared and inadequate when you insult and criticize me," rather than "You're always trying to be right."
3. "I feel like a little kid when you tell me what I should do," rather than "You're so controlling."

It is usually very important for the Adult Child to learn to communicate his *feelings* about another person's specific *behavior*, rather than repeating the dysfunctional pattern of simply blaming, insulting, shaming and rejecting.

We encourage this learning by asking clients to restate prejudicial or attacking statements whenever they are made in a general discussion. Often these statements *are* allowed as part of a general emotional release. However, they are *always* challenged if they are made to someone else in the group in an ordinary conversation.

We model this kind of communication when we confront inappropriate behavior in the group. We clearly describe the behavior and our own thoughts and/or feelings in response to it. It is often necessary to be very explicit that we are confronting the behavior, not the person, and that we still *like* the person we are confronting.

When a client is dealing with feelings about someone who is not present in the group, we will use a variety of methods to work with the issues. (See Chapters 8, and 12, "Working With Feelings", Parts 1 and 2, for a more detailed discussion.)

Rule Number Five

It's okay to make mistakes, people learn from mistakes.

Often clients report mistakes and then criticize themselves because they made the mistakes. Their attitude is often that mistakes are awful, irretrievable and unforgivable.

To reinforce the permission to make mistakes, we define a "mistake" in Child terms: "A mistake is when you do something that makes a mess you didn't mean to make; you'll probably have to do something about it, like apologize, clean it up or try to keep it from happening again."

To reinforce thinking clearly about mistakes, we usually ask a series of questions:

1. "What did you learn from the mistake?"
2. "Did you know that before?"
3. "Were you doing the best you could with the information you had?"
4. "What problems were created when the mistake was made?"
5. "Have you corrected the problems?"
6. "Would you forgive someone else who made that mistake?"
7. "Will you forgive yourself? If not, why not?"

If mistakes are made in group, we ask that they be corrected as soon as possible, usually immediately, and we acknowledge the client for recognizing and correcting the problem, or for letting it go, if that seems appropriate.

When we make mistakes, we acknowledge them openly and correct them if possible, or make amends if correction is not possible.

For example, we changed a group meeting time on short notice, and forgot to inform two people who were absent. When they missed group as a result, we offered to meet with them individually for an equivalent amount of time.

We sometimes encourage storytelling and sharing about "mistakes I have made", to demonstrate to the Inner Child that the world does not end when someone makes a mistake.

We keep a set of juggling blocks and an instruction manual *(Juggling For The Compleat Klutz)* in our group room. Clients who identify a need to get comfortable making mistakes are encouraged to practice juggling during the group. It is impossible to do this task without making mistakes. They are acknowledged randomly for both mistakes and successes.

Rule Number Six

Take your time, you don't have to hurry and it's okay for you to take as much time as you need.
Many Adult Children want to complete their therapy work instantly; this desire is usually a substitute behavior, created in response to the parental message to "hurry up and grow up". The work of healing the Inner Child takes time. We often state this and refuse contracts to do more than can reasonably be done in a period of time.

> **Laura:** *Tonight in group I want to be a baby and get strokes* (physical), *then be two and say* no, *then be four and ask questions and finally I want to talk about a problem at work.*
> **Therapist:** *What is really the most important to you?*
> **L:** *Getting strokes and talking about the problem at work.*
> **T:** *You'll probably have time to do those two things; ask someone for strokes now, and you can talk about the work problem later.* (We suspect that the need for strokes is connected to the work problem and to the highly agitated presentation.)

A client may display impatience while someone else is working, and may send the message for the other client or the therapist to hurry up. This is usually confronted:

1. If you want something for yourself, it's fine for you to find a way to get it, but not by discounting what someone else needs.
2. There's plenty to go around here; we (the therapists) are not the only source of support. Ask for what *you* want, rather than trying to get someone else to be different.
3. If you don't think he is working effectively, or is playing games, you can confront that.

Rule Number Seven

It's okay to get information from others; ask all the questions you want.

Adult Children often believe they should know things that they never had the opportunity to learn. Because children in dysfunctional families often do not learn how to ask for information, they become careful observers and attempt to figure things out for themselves.

When new clients just sit and observe the many activities in a busy group without ever asking any questions, we usually assume that we are seeing a dysfunctional pattern. We usually respond by assigning the client the task of asking frequent direct questions. Some people demonstrate this pattern indirectly, by revealing their assumptions and beliefs about what others are thinking or feeling. In that case, we challenge them by asking how they arrived at their information. We then suggest that they verify their information by asking questions. We often suggest specific questions to ask of others in the group. Examples include:

1. "Do you like me?" "Why?"
2. "What did you do to get over being scared of being here?"
3. "What would you do if your wife did that?"
4. "What would you do if I acted like a child in here?"
5. "What would you do if I showed the anger I feel inside?"

If appropriate, we also suggest questions to ask outside of the group, and sometimes suggest resource people who can answer questions.

Rule Number Eight

It's okay to ask for help.

Even thinking about asking for help can be difficult for an Adult Child who decided long ago that he not only had to do everything himself, he had to look like he didn't need help from anyone. Adult Children fear admitting "weakness".

We encourage asking in several different ways. One way is by identifying specific resources in the group.

Jack solved a similar problem a few months ago; ask him how he handled it. (As therapists, we also model asking each other for help in figuring out what to do or in getting out of sticky situations.)

Laurie questions, "Jon, we seem to be going around in circles with this problem. Will you listen and see where we're stuck?"

When someone in the group is looking as if he needs help, but not asking for it, others frequently get caught up in trying to help the person with the problem. Even if their help is useful, this tends to reinforce not asking, so we will often encourage clients to withhold help from each other unless it is asked for.

We often make a point of communicating that asking for help doesn't have to be grim and serious. One method of doing this is to model it.

Jon: Help!

Another method is to create playful exercises that can be used to practice asking for help.

Bea has agreed to stand in the middle of the room until she can convince other group members to hit her ten times with Nerf Balls (soft foam). First she giggles nervously and says, "I'm here." Nothing happens. Then she says, "I need to be hit ten times." Again, nothing happens. She picks up a ball and throws it at Jack, who throws it back and hits her with it. "That's one," she laughs.

Finally, Bea looks around the room at people and says, "Will you help me get out of the middle by throwing the Nerf Balls at me?" She is rapidly tagged with the remaining balls, and sits down, laughing, "That was fun!"

In addition to practicing in group, we talk with clients about how to ask family and friends for appropriate help, and we stroke them when they report on having done so. We remind them that even when they ask appropriately, others have the right to say *no*. It doesn't mean that there is something wrong with them if others say *no*.

Rule Number Nine

It's okay not to know everything; here are some ways to find out what you don't know . . .

Adult Children often believe that others know everything, and that there is something wrong with *them* because they lack information. We dispel this myth by telling them specifically that it's not true, asking where they learned what they know and openly sharing information about how others, including ourselves, learned what we know.

We also point out to them areas in which they know things that we *don't* know. This is sometimes a shock to Adult Children, who think that if they do know something, then everyone else obviously must know it, too — and it couldn't be very important, anyway.

We encourage asking for information and instruction, within and outside of the group. Sometimes we have clients bring model airplanes to group in order to experience learning to put them together with help. Others have used their time in group to learn and practice study skills, project planning, time management skills, etc.

Rule Number Ten

Your own needs and feelings are the first thing for you to think about; then pay attention to the needs and feelings of others.

The active group situation offers many circumstances in which the Adult Child, who learned to be a helpful rescuer, can attempt to put his own needs and feelings aside while helping others. When we see this behavior we confront it. We ask the client what he was wanting for himself when he had the impulse to be helpful.

A client passes some homemade cookies around the group. When the bag comes to *Sara*, who mothered her seven siblings, she automatically counts the cookies to make sure there will be enough for everyone if she takes one. We call it to her attention, and she cries and admits that she could never have anything she wanted until everyone else was cared for. She also recognizes that she is still doing that in her current life, and, by doing so, is inviting others to discount her needs.

We ask people to interrupt their automatic helping behavior to see if it is a substitute behavior. We invite them to see if they are giving away what they really want for themselves, hoping someone else will figure it out and give them what they want. If this is the case, we encourage them to ask directly for what they want. Others can then respond to their requests and say what their own needs or wants are in the situation.

Rule Number Eleven

Playing and laughing is fun, and fun is good!

Opportunities for playful behavior arise frequently during each group. We play with words, Nerf Balls, ideas, stuffed animals and many other things. Laughter is encouraged, but "gallows humor" (laughing about something that is painful) is *always* confronted. For example,

> **Nikki** (Laughing): *Well, that guy who said he wanted to go out with me didn't call.*
> **Therapist:** *That doesn't sound funny; it sounds like you feel hurt.*
> **N** (Crying): *I really wanted him to call. I was trying not to feel the pain.*
> **T:** *It's not a good idea to invite other people to laugh with you at your pain; it makes it worse. This is a safe place to show how you really feel.*

Rule Number Twelve

It is okay to say *no* here; you can refuse to do something if you don't want to do it.

Sometimes Adult Children are afraid to experiment with behavior that would have caused problems in the past. They agree to do something and then don't do it. We ask why they didn't complete their agreement, and, if they give excuses, we suggest they say aloud, "I don't want to do it." We then congratulate them for taking the risk of saying *no* and suggest they practice doing it in the group. They usually comply, timidly at first, then with increasing enthusiasm.

Clients are encouraged to pay attention to their own needs and feelings before deciding whether to say *yes* or *no* to another client's request. If they do say *no,* we ask them to state the reason for it, eg., "I'm tired," or "I'm involved in my own work right now," etc. The client making the request is encouraged to ask someone else. Usually *someone* will respond.

Rule Number Thirteen

This is a safe place to try out new and unfamiliar behavior; others will accept it, especially if you ask for their support and tell them what you are going to do (so that they can respond to you appropriately).

Clients make agreements or "contracts" to practice new behaviors such as saying *no,* asking questions, asking for physical strokes (eg., back rubs, hugs, being held), asking to be read to, etc. During the contracting process at the beginning of each group, they ask for the cooperation of others to meet those requests or to otherwise support their new behavior. If someone doesn't want to cooperate, she says so at that time. It is understood that if a request is denied, the reason for the denial will be explained, and that the request should be made of someone else.

Rule Number Fourteen

It's okay for you to ask directly for what you want and need; you and others are expected to do so, and you don't have to take care of others by guessing at what they want.

Many Adult Children look and act needy in the group and hope someone will notice and take care of them. We comment on this behavior when we see it, and encourage them to state what they want and ask for it. Examples include:

1. The asking words are "Will you . . ." not "I wish . . ." or "I want . . ." or "I'd like . . ."
2. "Will you pass me the tissues?"
3. You are looking like you need strokes; ask someone for them. Pick whomever you want, and say, "Will you put your arm around me, hug me, hold me, or whatever would feel good to your Child."

We encourage anyone who thinks they know what someone else wants to ask the other person, rather than automatically giving what they assume the other person wants.

Rule Number Fifteen

No violence or threats of violence are permitted.

It is important, of course, to discuss violent impulses and to problem-solve about how to deal with the feelings that produce them, without carrying them out. It may be important to express those thoughts and impulses in a controlled way, like beating on pillows, but only after a clear agreement is made to do so, and appropriate protection is arranged. (See Chapters 8 and 12, "Working With Feelings", Parts I and II, for a more detailed discussion of this process.)

Rule Number Sixteen

Tobacco, alcohol and nonprescription drugs are not permitted in the treatment environment. The use of prescription medication needs to be monitored.

These potentially destructive chemicals divert attention from the problems of the Inner Child and cause problems of their own. If someone comes to group under the influence of drugs or alcohol, they are permitted to stay, but are not allowed to participate in any of the group activities. Smoking is never allowed; in addition to the physical and chemical effects, smoking in the group setting is almost always a form of agitation, and should be confronted as a substitute behavior.

Special Notes For Therapists

Permission for a client to love and accept his Inner Child can be effective when it comes from someone who loves and accepts his own Inner Child. A therapist will have difficulty giving a client effective permission to do something the therapist does not allow himself to do. Providing corrective parenting for a client's Inner Child requires the therapist to present congruent messages from all three Ego States. The therapist's Parent must approve of the permission. His Adult must know how to use the permissions himself. His Child must accept the permission and obey it.

Therapists who have not yet healed their own Inner Child traumas will have a hard time getting clients to accept permissions that they have not accepted themselves. Even if the work is technically correct, the client will sense the incongruity. Because the client is rarely in a position to confront the therapist's incongruities, he will just have one more experience that feels unsafe to talk about.

Because many therapists have unresolved Inner Child issues, scrupulous honesty is the best protection for everyone concerned. It is useful to say to a client, "I can help you think about that issue (eg., taking time to play), but I haven't solved it very well for myself. Do you know someone who has solved it? Can you talk to that person about her beliefs and activities?" It is useful to work with a co-therapist whose strengths are complementary to yours.

No therapist is perfect, just as no parent is perfect. When a therapist does corrective parenting, we recommend ongoing consultation or supervision. Everyone has blind spots and everyone has sore spots. Use feedback from clients as well as peers to guide your own continued growth. We have experienced the phenomenon that, as soon as we resolve a problem in our own personal therapy, several clients present that problem to us in the next week. Many of our clients who are therapists have reported similar experiences.

Special Note For The Adult Child Who Is Seeking Corrective Parenting

In order to be an appropriate model and teacher for your Inner Child, your therapist must be open and honest about how she takes care of her own Inner Child. She should be able to nurture her own Inner Child while providing a safe space for you to learn and grow. Seeing the therapist taking care of herself reassures your Inner Child that the therapist is not like your parent(s) — you don't have to take care of her.

The rules and restrictions you received from your parents had power over you because you needed your parents' protection, support, etc. You were too young to provide these for yourself, and it was the threat of losing those things that gave them power over you. Even though you do not need those things from your parents today, your Inner Child still believes you do; and that is why you are reluctant to disobey the old rules.

It takes courage to use your relationship with your therapist to temporarily stand in place of the relationship you had with your parents. You may use your therapist as a temporary substitute parent to teach your Inner Child that you are lovable and capable, and teach you to honor and protect that small part of you, until you can learn to get needs met directly. Because the therapist is not really your parent, and because your relationship with the therapist is entirely voluntary, **the only person who has the power to make you listen to the new permissions is you.**

Your therapist will help you learn to recognize that you cannot change the past, that you must grieve for it and move on. **As you learn to allow the Inner Child to feel, to talk and to trust, you will learn to love yourself without loving only yourself, and to care about others without caring only about others.**

CHAPTER 8

Working with Feelings — Part 1

Paula still feels depressed, long after the end of a relationship. She complains about how bad she feels, but seems intent on proving that she has a right to feel bad. She does not seem to be grieving or letting go; she is obsessed, hanging on to something that is irretrievably gone.

When her pattern of getting repetitively stuck in her bad feelings is pointed out, she reacts by feeling blamed and by angrily accusing us of being insensitive and uncaring.

When we ask her about similar feelings in the past, Paula reports that she felt this way when she was 14, when her mother died of cancer. A controlling and hysterical aunt had accused her of being responsible for her mother's death. Encouraged to repeat (to an imaginary image of her aunt) "I'm angry at you," Paula moves rapidly into an important phase of grief work, feeling and expressing anger — first at her aunt, then at her mother for dying. This, in turn, helps her remember and express even earlier anger at her mother for being cold, distant and unavailable.

When a client expresses a feeling, we will sometimes respond with nurturing support and understanding, inviting the client to continue with the feeling and to go more deeply into it. This is especially true when we are working with someone who has difficulty being aware of her feelings.

Frequently, we will ask the person to stay in touch with the feeling, while trying to remember the earliest time she felt the same way. **When the feelings seem out of proportion to the current situation,** this strategy often helps the person remember the events that originally created the feelings.

Sometimes we will respond by apparently ignoring the feeling, by responding only to the content or by asking the person to think about something (what kind of response they want, for example). Sometimes we will respond by providing information about feelings and other times we will actively insist that the client stop trying to control others with his feelings.

The major factors that determine how we will respond to feelings are: (1) the client's goals and (2) our assessment of whether or not the client's expression of feelings is a *substitute behavior* (see Chapter 4).

Taking the client's goals into consideration helps to keep us from making the mistake of assuming that the same procedures are appropriate for all problems. One client may be coming to therapy, for example, because he recognizes that he is being run by emotions, whereas another may want to work on the problem of being out of touch with her feelings.

The possibility that the client may be engaging in substitute behavior must be considered, because the therapist's task is to help the client to attend to the real needs that underly the substitutes.

Although feelings and emotions are a natural part of being human, the methods of expressing them are learned. In a healthy family, children eventually learn to be able to feel emotions and to think about what to do about them, at the same time.

Bobby, four, has lost his dime in his toybox; he is standing next to the box, screaming.

> **Father:** *I see you're upset; what are you upset about?*
> **Bobby** (through the tears): *Lost my dime in there!*
> **Father:** *And you want it back?* (Bobby nods.) *Well, you can stand there and cry, you can take things out of the box and look for it or you can ask someone to help you. What do you want to do?*

Bobby is learning that he can think while he is upset and that he can use his ability to think to help him solve the problem he is upset about.

People who grow up in dysfunctional families are not likely to learn effective ways of thinking about their feelings; as a result, feelings become distorted and exaggerated. People do not get angry and use the energy to solve a problem; they shout, scream, break things and/or hurt people. People do not just feel sad, grieve, let go and move forward; they get depressed, withdrawn and nonfunctional for days or weeks at a time. People do not express fear and get reassurance and support; they get panicky and hysterical, insisting that their fear is the only relevant consideration in the situation.

The Adult Child who grows up in this kind of setting will develo a variety of problems centering around the expression and use of feelings. The severity of the problems will vary, depending on the particular pattern in the family.

Awareness Of Feelings

In extreme circumstances, Adult Children completely shut down their awareness of any feelings.

Dorothy couldn't tell us about any of her feelings when her estranged husband returned, wanted to move back in and offered to go into therapy with her. However, she did go home and attempt suicide.

When *Don's* wife threatens to leave because he acts like a wooden robot around the house, he agrees to come to therapy. In the therapy session, he has nothing that he wants or wants to change about himself, and doesn't understand why his behavior should be a problem for his wife.

Ned, an executive, doesn't have any "feelings" about the stress on his job. He *does* feel the pain of a duodenal ulcer.

Feelings That Are Approved

Some Adult Children learn only to feel the feelings that are "approved" for their assigned role in the family.

Dad, the alcoholic, feels angry (but no one else is allowed to feel angry), and Mom feels sad. When **Deena** was a child in this family, she was responded to when she felt scared or sad, but not if she was mad. As an adult, she expects others to take care of her when she

whines and acts scared. She behaves this way instead of being direct
with her anger.

Feelings To Manipulate Others

Some learn to use feelings to manipulate others.

Paula was *taught* to manipulate by having her feelings repeatedly
ignored until she became hysterically upset. Her outbursts would
often succeed in getting someone to give in grudgingly to what she
wanted, but she would then be told that she shouldn't be upset
because she was causing the problem herself by being so emotional.
Typically, she was then isolated from the rest of the family until she
could learn to "behave (control) herself".

Paula's family rule of "Don't Feel" did not actually prevent her
from having feelings; it merely taught her that some feelings are
useful for manipulation and control, and that ordinary expressions of
feeling are to be ignored. She learned that, in order to get any
response to her feelings, she had to exaggerate them out of
proportion. She didn't learn that **feelings are internal signals that can
be used to direct and guide appropriate behavior.**

Paula's childhood hysteria finally got a response — a negative
response seemed to be preferable to no response at all. She is furious
at us when we are not impressed with her hysteria and keep insisting
that she get on with her grief work.

Self-Criticism And Self-Judgment

**Some Adult Children do feel, but criticize and judge themselves
mercilessly for having or expressing the feelings.** They think of
themselves as stupid, childish, weak, etc. This, of course, produces
more feelings in response to the criticism, which they respond to
with more self-criticism.

Most learn to pay close attention to the feelings of *others*, often by
picking up subtle clues and mind-reading. They focus on taking care
of the other person's feelings, often at their own expense. They may
arbitrarily decide what the other's feelings are, and then respond to
those "feelings" with either caretaking or rejection. The motivation
behind this pattern is often to protect themselves from negative
feelings of others.

Co-dependents need *permission, information* and *modeling* in
order to learn what is naturally learned by children who grow up in

healthy families. When we provide these things for clients, we are consciously replacing the parental messages about feelings that they have been following all their lives.

Co-dependents may need to learn:

1. That they *have* feelings
2. How to think about their own feelings
3. What feelings are for
4. How to express their feelings effectively to help them get what they need in the world

Permission To Feel

Verbal permission alone will not convince the Inner Child who believes otherwise that it is safe to feel and express feelings. The therapist must respond to the hints that a client is feeling, by gently calling attention to the glistening eyes, the shaky voice, the sudden frozen posture, instead of politely ignoring what the client is uncomfortable about revealing openly. Some clients accept this invitation to share feelings; others may feel assaulted by it, and angrily reject the therapist's observation, insisting "I'm just fine!"

When Paula is shouting and beating a pillow with a padded bat, *Kathy,* a new client, sits with a smile frozen onto her face. I send an experienced client to sit next to Kathy and explain how terrified he felt the first time he saw anger work in the group. He, like many Adult Children, would do almost anything to avoid an angry confrontation. Kathy listens, taking in the nurturing support. Soon, the memories come flooding back: overhearing her parents shouting, while she is blocking her bedroom door to protect her little sisters from her father's crazy outbursts. She cries, beginning to release the tears and grief of a lost childhood.

More than just talking about it, the actual events of the group gradually convince the Adult Child that it is safe to share feelings in the group. She sees other clients expressing and releasing strong feelings, and sees that nothing bad happens to them. We ask her to notice that she feels more accepting of and closer to others after they show their feelings, and point out that others would probably feel the same toward her. She sees others talk about how they feel in response to each other, and notices that those feelings are acknowledged, rather than ignored. She sees people, especially the therapist, actively seek out and invite the open expression of emotion, in response to minimal cues that someone is feeling something.

Sometimes permission is given through confrontation of passive behavior (see Chapter 4).

When **Martha** tears a tissue to shreds (agitation) while insisting she has nothing to work on, we call her attention to her hands, and remind her how her passivity invites us either to think for her or to discount her. We ask her to pay attention to what she is trying not to feel. She starts to cry about her separation from her children.

In a safe setting, feelings tend to be contagious. When one person in a group expresses long-repressed feelings, others tend to "catch it". Exposure to other clients' intense expression of feelings stimulates some Adult Children to acknowledge their own. Keeping groups ongoing and contractual, rather than time-limited and formally structured, is a way of insuring that clients will "catch" feelings from each other. Experienced clients have learned the importance of expressing feelings and do so freely. Newcomers are often shocked and frightened at these intense expressions. We find it necessary to provide caring support for newcomers during the first few group sessions. A buddy system is helpful, where an experienced client or a therapy assistant sits with and explains things to the new member. We always urge newcomers to ask questions, but Adult Children, who follow the dysfunctional family rule of "Don't Talk", do not easily accept the permission.

Kate sits through two groups, looking aloof, cool and distant. In her third group, she agrees to discuss a problem. The group is active and busy. She sits on the sidelines, although we invite her into several conversations. Five minutes before the group is to end, she rushes from the room, saying "I can't get what I need here!" When I lead her back in the room, she recognizes that she is finally experiencing the frustration she felt as a child, when her parents were "too busy" to respond to her. The perceived similarity to her early life experiences finally pierced the armor of frozen feelings, and we could start to work. Because time was short, we agreed to continue that work in the next session. Part of the work will be to give her information about what to do when she feels a need for attention.

A client can also experience permission to feel when asked to engage in a childlike behavior he finds difficult to do — often because such behaviors were forbidden or dangerous. Here we may need to confront the family message of "Don't Trust", by asking the client to observe what actually happens to others when they engage in similar behaviors. We demonstrate our trustworthiness by making clear that we are not pushing the client into the behaviors, but will wait without pressure until he is willing to make an agreement to do the activity.

Sam agrees to ask people to do things for him (get his coffee, hand him something, tell him something, sit with an arm around him, etc.).

Marilyn, who grew up in a very repressive family, agrees to ask questions that a four-year-old might ask about why and how things happen, eg., "Why is that man crying? Are you gonna spank her?"

Tina agrees to say *no,* out loud.

Jack agrees to stand in the middle of the room and ask everyone to pay attention to him.

All of these behaviors, and many others that are described in other chapters, can be seen as natural behaviors that a spontaneous, healthy child would easily do.

When people engage in the previously forbidden or dangerous behavior, they are likely to experience feelings and memories connected to the events that led to the suppression of those natural behaviors.

Information About Feelings

Once Co-dependents become aware of and begin to express their feelings, they need information about what their feelings mean and what to do about them. During therapy sessions, we give this information directly, when we observe the client behaving as if he doesn't know it.

Because any conversation about feelings is likely to be taboo in a dysfunctional family, few Adult Children have any cognitive information about sources, meanings, uses or limitations of feelings. Although information in books is helpful, it is far more impelling to give someone the information personally, especially while they are actually feeling the emotion.

We have found that Adult Children often need the following specific information:

1. There are reasons for feelings.
2. Feelings usually have specific meanings; when the meanings are understood, the feelings can be used as signals to indicate what needs to be done.
3. It is possible to think and feel at the same time.

4. Feelings don't make things happen, but sometimes expressions of feelings lead to a response.

We often spend significant amounts of time in the therapy sessions giving people this information. In the following sections, we indicate what we actually say directly to our clients.

There Are Reasons For Feelings

When *Kathy* starts to sob about her experience of terror when she listened to her parents fighting, we tell her, "It is normal and okay to feel scared in that situation; you are feeling sad now because you didn't get the protection you needed when you were little."

When *Jan* recounts, in an angry voice, the story of waiting for her father for hours outside the tavern, we tell her she sounds angry, and that most people would feel angry if they were expected to do that. Jan was surprised that she sounded angry, and also surprised that anger was being accepted as a normal feeling — she thought that feeling angry was a sign that there was something wrong with her.

When *Connie* returned to group two weeks after her father's funeral, she thought there was something seriously wrong with her because she still thought and cried about her father. We explained that it is normal for sad feelings to persist for a long time after a major loss. She was surprised and relieved. With that reassurance, she went through a normal grieving process.

Simply giving information about normal feelings, labeling them and explaining what they mean and why they occur, can be enormously helpful to an Adult Child.

Feelings Usually Have Specific Meanings

When the meanings of feelings are understood, these feelings can be used as signals to indicate what needs to be done.

Feelings are like the signal lights on the dashboard of your car; they tell you that there is something going on that needs your attention. The signal is not the problem, and if you ignore the signal, the problem that produced it will probably get worse. When you act appropriately on the signal, the feeling will change and go away.

Anger

Anger is energy to get a problem solved. It's like the energy you use to pull harder on a door when it is stuck, or to tell someone to get off your foot if they are stepping on it. You can use the angry energy to motivate you to think about what to do to solve the problem, and to do it. The anger goes away when the problem gets solved, or when you really give up trying to solve it. (See the section on Sadness in this chapter.)

Many Adult Children are terrified of anger, whether it is their own or others'. As children, they witnessed distorted, destructive, often violent expressions of anger, and have no models for using anger in a problem-solving way.

Laura was angry because her son was being very noisy when she needed to concentrate on intellectual work. She kept trying to ignore the problem, because she was afraid that if she let herself get angry, she would express it in the abusive and insulting way she had seen in her family. The longer she tried to ignore the problem, the angrier she got, and the more frightened she became of what she would do.

Once she understood the source of her fears and beliefs about anger, and took the permission to think about what to do about her feeling, it was easy for her to solve the problem with her son. She made an agreement to spend time with him before and after she did her work, and for him to watch TV quietly, with earphones, while she worked.

When you are angry at someone, the appropriate thing to do about it is to tell her that you are angry; it's okay to *sound* angry when you tell her. Tell the person specifically what she did that you're angry about, why you are angry about it and what you want her to do about it — apologize, make amends, clean up the mess, do something different in the future, etc. Use your anger to get something useful to happen. When you feel satisfied with the response, your anger should be gone.

Not everyone you do this with will respond to you the way you would like: she may ignore you, get angry back, tell you that you're bad for being angry, or use your anger as an excuse not to respond to you. You will have to decide what to do about each situation. You may have to tell the person what you will do if she doesn't respond. Don't do this if you are not willing to follow through on it. After you get skilled and comfortable at this, and someone consistently fails to respond to you, think about why you want to maintain a relationship with someone who behaves as if she don't care about how you feel.

Elly is angry at her husband. She has a professional office in her home. Her husband, who was fired from his job almost a year ago, keeps himself too busy to look for a job by "helping" her with the office work — frequently leaving important things undone. She whines at him about his poor work, and ineffectively nags him to get a job. She gets support to tell him directly that she is angry about what he is doing. When his behavior doesn't change, she hires someone to do the office work, and tells him that they are cutting back on entertainment in order to cover the expense. He is now actively looking for work.

Fear

When someone is afraid, or concerned about fear, we give the following information: **Fear means that you need information or reassurance, so that you can have some idea of what's going to happen. It is a signal that you are off-balance, because something is different from the way it was a moment ago, or from the way you expected it to be. The difference isn't necessarily dangerous; it's like the feeling you get in the elevator when it starts to drop. The feeling goes away when you get information or reassurance, so that you can get your balance back.**

It's very important to know that being afraid doesn't mean something is wrong with *you*. It just means that you need something. The thing to do about being afraid is to do something about getting the information or help you need.

Sam was always on guard. He "knew" that if he did anything wrong, his mother would get hysterical and his father would get drunk, critical and abusive. He believed he was in control of what happened in the family and lived in constant fear that he would make a mistake. He carried this fear into his adult life. He tried so hard to control people that he could never relax and always felt tension in his abdomen, which often developed into pain.

When we suggested that in some circumstances he could ask people about what they planned to do next, he became quite frightened. He practiced this new behavior in group until he became comfortable with it, and then started using it at work. His physical distress diminished.

In most cases, the information you need when you're scared has to come from outside you; you usually have to tell *someone* that you are scared. Trying to handle it all by yourself, without even telling anyone, usually means just trying to turn off the part of you that's scared. It's like locking the scared Child inside you in a closet, rather than taking care of him.

Kathy, the new client described earlier, still felt scared when others did intense anger work in group. After getting the above information, however, and observing for herself that no one was actually getting hurt, she was able to respond to her own fear by asking someone to sit close to her. She was pleased to discover that she had the power to do something to get nurturing for her Inner Child.

When you are afraid, it usually means that you think something bad is going to happen. It helps to ask yourself what that is. Then you can see if that thing is really likely to happen in this specific situation, or if you are remembering something that happened in another situation. When you know what you are afraid of will happen, you can also think about what you could do about it if it really did happen.

You *can* think when you're afraid, so that you can think about what you need and what you can do to get it. You can also do things even though you are afraid; you don't have to be immobilized by the fear. Many times the fear goes away only *after* you do the scary thing and discover that nothing bad really happened. If you try to wait for the fear to go away before you act, you may have to wait a very long time.

Karen, a manager, was afraid to confront her boss about his ineffective supervision of her — ignoring her completely unless there was something wrong.

When we helped her to think about what she was scared of, rather than just feeling about it, she realized that she was reacting to her boss the way she did to her father, who had treated her the same way. When she thought about it, she also realized there were many things about her boss that were different from her father, including the fact that she had seen him respond appropriately to feedback.

She asked for a meeting with her boss and told him what she needed from him in order to be more effective in her job. She reported back that the interview went very well and that her boss was changing his behavior with her.

Sadness

When someone is sad — or trying or pretending not to be sad — we give the following advice: Sad is what you feel when you have lost something or someone that was important to you, when nothing you can do or say can get back what you lost. Sad is about giving up and letting go, and feeling the hurt and loss of not having the important thing or person anymore. When we feel sad, we are telling ourselves that there is someone or something we need to say goodbye to. You have to feel sad about what is gone before you can really take in something or someone new.

You don't really need to do anything about feeling sad; just let yourself feel it when it comes up. If you don't try to stop it, it will come up by itself; you will feel it for a while, and then it will subside. It will come back again at another time, probably when something reminds you of the loss.

Between times, you can go on about your business and feel okay. After a while, the feelings will be less strong when they come, and they will come less often. It may be a very long time before they go away completely, if they ever do.

Some Adult Children often have a very difficult time acknowledging loss and often cover the sadness with other feelings.

Paula's Inner Child believed that if only she could get hysterical enough, her mother would still be alive. Rationally, of course, she knows, in her Adult Ego State, that her mother is irretrievably dead, but her emotional Child led her to repeatedly engage in relationships where she got hysterical when her partner threatened to go away. She was often "successful" in intimidating the partner to respond to the emotional blackmail, but each one would eventually leave.

When she expressed her Child's rage at her mother for leaving, Paula was finally able to experience her sadness.

Some Adult Children want to feel their sadness in private. It is important to encourage them to share this feeling with at least one other person; they need to know that they can be accepted, even though they are feeling bad and not looking perfect. (A more detailed discussion of the issue of grief and loss can be found in Chapter 15.)

Happiness

Most Adult Children believe that happiness is some kind of reward, a prize they might earn some day if they work hard enough, sacrifice enough, take care of other people enough or are "good" enough. They do not have the information that happiness is a side effect of being true to themselves and getting what they need. Happy feelings can range from the quiet satisfaction of getting what you need to the exuberant celebration of success or of unexpected abundance.

Nothing needs to be done about happy feelings; they are simply to be enjoyed. Many Adult Children fear feeling happy, convinced that they will "pay for it" later on. They have concluded that feeling good "makes" something bad happen.

When *Marjie* was small, the spontaneous joy she experienced when she accomplished something invoked ridicule from her father and brothers. Now, if she is doing well at work, she feels compelled to do things that undercut her effectiveness, like not returning customers' calls. In therapy, she practices bragging to the group about her accomplishments, and getting positive recognition for them, especially from the men. She is gradually learning that feeling good doesn't have to "make" bad things happen. We also explain to her Child that, in the normal course of events, things change (days, seasons, etc.), that change is natural and that good and bad things may happen and follow one another, but that they do not necessarily cause one another.

It Is Possible To Think And Feel At The Same Time

In dysfunctional families, children observe and learn the exact opposite. They rarely see anyone thinking about feelings.

Abbie comes to group and says that she thinks Laurie is a bitch and is scared to talk to her, confusing Laurie with her own abusive, withholding mother. Jon asks Abbie a series of questions, designed to help her identify the source of the feelings:

Q: *Have you ever felt this way before?*
A: *Yes, with a female boss.*
Q: *Before that? In school?*
A: *Yes, with a female teacher.*
Q: *When you were little?*
A: *Yes, with Mother.*
Q: *What's the earliest time you can remember feeling the same way?*
A: *When I asked Mother where Daddy was and she went into another room and wouldn't speak to me for three days.*

By answering the questions (thinking) while continuing to feel the feelings, Abbie gradually breaks down the barrier between her Child and the grown-up part of herself. She recognizes the source of her feelings, and moves into doing something direct to release them. She imagines, with our support, that her mother is in the group room, and tells her, with appropriate feeling, about her fear and anger.

Bonnie can remember the events surrounding her father's death, but can't get in touch with her grief and her fear and anger about being left with an abusive mother. We encourage her, as homework, to write a letter to her dead father, telling him what happened to her during his final illness and immediately after his death. She reports feeling sad and crying while she was writing the letter, and floods of tears come as she reads the letter aloud in group. Finally, we have her write the letter she would have wanted her father to write in response. She does so, and experiences great relief when she recognizes that it is really herself nurturing her own Child.

Feelings Don't Make Things Happen

Although feelings don't make things happen, sometimes expressions of feelings lead to a response.

Feelings aren't discussed in dysfunctional homes. Children naturally believe in their own omnipotence, and in dysfunctional families, they tend to blame themselves for the problems in the family. More specifically, children in dysfunctional families often come to believe that it is their *feelings* that cause various events to occur.

Jenny thought that feeling scared brought on abuse; she learned to turn off the scare and act tough. It never occurred to her, until we talked about it, that it was her tough behavior, not her control of her feelings, that kept her relatively safe.

Nikki was afraid to let herself feel good. Every time she felt good, her mother became abusive. Her mother also became abusive when Nikki felt angry, sad or scared; but somehow she magically associated feeling good with being hurt later.

Sarah thought that feeling scared would automatically cause someone to help her. She learned to act like a victim when she was scared, and people did help. She learned in a group that asking for help directly was far more effective and felt better than whining.

Adult Children need to learn that appropriately expressing feelings to people who can help solve the problems is likely to bring positive results; in any case, it is far better than either magically avoiding or exaggerating certain feelings.

It often comes as a surprise to Adult Children that, when they express their negative feelings in a way that gets an appropriate response, the negative feelings dissolve, transforming into relief, peacefulness and happiness.

Feelings Are Not The Only Things That Are Important

Not only are feelings important, but thoughts and behavior are important.

Adult Children who become skilled at denying their own feelings do not learn an appropriate range of response to those feelings. When they *do* allow feelings to emerge, they often experience those feelings with such urgency that they feel compelled to act on them immediately. They may make sudden, apparently irrational decisions, based exclusively on their newly-found feelings.

Shirley asked a friend for a favor, and the friend went to considerable inconvenience to meet Shirley's schedule. Later, Shirley decided she felt bad about something the friend had said, and cancelled their meeting at the last minute. Her friend was furious, and Shirley became angry at the friend, who "didn't understand".

Shirley did this over and over in her life, about large and small issues. Shirley spent twelve years in a Co-dependent relationship. At the end of her first couple's treatment session, both partners made another appointment to work together on the relationship. That night, Shirley realized how badly she had been feeling for the past eight years. She moved out of their jointly owned home, and locked her partner out of their jointly owned business. She reported that she "couldn't stand" to be with him another minute. The resulting complications took several months and several lawyers to straighten out.

It is important for Adult Children to learn that although feelings are one important source of information, other sources should be considered as well.

Shirley's pattern is first to make decisions without considering her feelings at all, then to change the decisions abruptly when the feelings finally do emerge. She agrees that her life would progress more smoothly if she were to take into account other people's needs and feelings, relevant aspects of the general situation *and* her feelings, before she makes any decision.

This is difficult for her to do, because she either thinks and acts, or feels and acts. She needs to learn both to *think and* to *feel* before taking any action.

The following process can help Adult Children learn to think and feel at the same time. We taught Shirley first to notice when she wasn't paying attention to her feelings, and to then ask herself the question, "How do I feel about this?" We suggested that she not make a firm decision if she couldn't answer the question.

To help her learn to recognize her feelings, we taught her to notice what visceral sensations occurred when she felt angry (for her, a tightening across her shoulders), scared (a fluttering in her abdomen) or sad (a sensation of pressure behind her eyes). Using the body sensations she learned to label her feelings. Then she learned to think about what stimulated the feeling. Sometimes it was a current situation and other times it was a feeling stimulated by the similarity of the current situation to one that had happened in the past. For example, when she heard a raised voice, it reminded her of the overwhelming fear when her father shouted at her.

Separating currently stimulated feelings from feelings that are attached to past events helps an Adult Child decide what can be done about the feeling at the moment. We reminded Shirley of what feelings were for, and what she could do when she felt any uncomfortable feeling.

Next we encouraged her to think about what would be most likely to happen if she expressed that feeling in the specific situation. We asked her to notice whether she was in an environment that was likely to be responsive or unresponsive to her needs and her expression of feelings. Based on her assessment of the situation, she learned to choose among several alternatives for dealing with her feelings. She might go ahead and ask for what she needed, ask for nurturing or ask for somebody to change something. She might decide to wait until another time to deal with the feeling, to delay making a decision until the feeling was resolved or to resolve the feeling in a therapy session by dealing with something that had happened in the past.

Teaching Shirley how to pay attention to her feelings when she was discounting them, allowed her to integrate feeling and thinking. As a result, she no longer needed to act impulsively on the feelings when they did come to her awareness.

Modeling

If therapists don't take care of their own feelings appropriately, they continue sending the messages "Don't Feel" or "Don't Show Your Feelings" to their clients. If we practice what we preach, our clients really believe it's okay for them to take the risk of showing their feelings, too.

I *(Laurie)* told the group that Jane, someone they were all very concerned about, had decided abruptly to terminate her therapy. I explained how I used all my skill, to no avail, to persuade her to change her decision. My own anger and sadness were just beneath the surface. Everyone stayed calm and rational. I then said that

I needed to do something about my own feelings, before I could do effective therapy with the group.

I talked about my anger at Jane for breaking her agreement and my frustration at not being skilled enough to help her. Group members asked questions and talked about their anger at being "abandoned" by Jane. Then Jon asked me what I needed. I started to cry and realized that I needed to be sad — there was nothing further I could do, and it was time to give up and let go. As I cried, others shed tears. We all hugged, then relaxed for a while and got on with the rest of the work. After my work, one client said, "You are really different from my mom; you're really telling the truth about your feelings."

Whenever we model taking care of our own feelings, we get feedback from clients about how much they learn. "I asked *Jon* if he was sad. He said *yes*, and told me what he was sad about (a good friend moving away). He told me that I didn't have to do anything to help fix it. When I tried to help, he told me that he needed to feel sad until he was finished with the feeling. He really meant it!

Whenever we model healthy responses to confrontation, instead of inappropriate or angry responses, clients report astonishment and relief. "When *Laurie* disagreed with what Jon wanted to do, I kept waiting for him to get really mad and hit her. He didn't. He asked why she disagreed. They actually talked about it and decided what to do — together. I could hardly believe it; part of me is still waiting for him to get back at her!"

Demonstrating appropriate self-care to clients is an extremely powerful way to give them permission to change their Co-dependent patterns of handling feelings. By using the modeling, as well as the actual information we present, the Inner Child can learn healthy ways of recognizing and expressing ordinary feelings.

CHAPTER 9

DIAGNOSING DEVELOPMENTAL DYSFUNCTIONS: HOW OLD IS THE INNER CHILD?

Roxy is extremely judgmental and critical of herself, finding fault with almost anything she does. We ask her to hold a small pillow and imagine that it is herself, as a newborn (our idea is to get her to recognize her basic "okayness"). She begins to cry, then says, "You shouldn't be here! You should never have been born!" She throws the pillow across the room and cries hysterically.

Her treatment of her own Inner Child mirrors the conditions Roxy experienced as an infant. We now see evidence that her problems began at birth, and we can define one of the goals of her treatment as finding a way for her Inner Child to experience accepting and nurturing transactions with others.

Most of the basic problems of the Co-dependent can be

understood by examining the developmental stages of childhood. At each stage, there are specific things that the child needs to do, and specific transactions that need to occur between the child and the caretakers, if the child is to become an adult who functions effectively in the world. When these transactions do not take place, corrective parenting can help the Adult Child fill in the missing pieces.

To provide corrective parenting experiences, the therapist needs to assess the approximate age of the Inner Child and to understand the developmental and transactional needs and abilities of a child of that age. In this chapter, we will describe some of the clues we use to recognize a developmental problem and to assign a corresponding stage to it. In the following chapters, we describe each developmental stage in detail, showing the critical transactions for each stage, appropriate parenting and the inadequate parenting that often occurs in dysfunctional families. We will also discuss specific treatment techniques for healing the problems that can be created in each stage.

Questions To Ask In Developmental Diagnosis

Developmental diagnosis is not a simple process of matching the client's symptoms and problems against a checklist. There are several key questions that need to be answered in order to recognize a pattern that may be characteristic of a specific developmental stage.

1. "What does the Inner Child need that he is not getting?"
2. "How does the person go about trying to meet that need?"
3. "What prevents the person from being effective in getting the need met?"

The answers to these questions are essential to the corrective parenting approach to treatment. We need them answered in order to determine what kind of transactions to create or prescribe for the client, so that his Inner Child can experience the developmental learning that was missed.

Roxy identified an archaic need for unconditional positive strokes, a need to be told that it was okay for her to be alive. When we tested her ability to nurture her own infant Inner Child, we discovered that she couldn't do it. Her Parent Ego State was incorporated from her original parents, who didn't want her. In order to be healed, her Inner Child needs the experience of being welcomed and nurtured as a newborn infant. She also probably needs direct nurturing at every subsequent stage of development before she can learn to nurture herself appropriately.

In making a developmental diagnosis, we are not following a logical, sequential process; rather, we are trying to match patterns. The process is very much like a game that used to appear in *The Saturday Evening Post* magazine. The reader is shown a small circular portion of a road map that contains some highway numbers, portions of city names and occasional landmarks or monuments. There is enough partial information to allow a well-informed person to figure out specifically where they are in the United States.

Sometimes we ask the client directly: "What does your Child need?" At other times, we use the question theoretically, to guide our own thinking. Sometimes we expect a direct answer from the client; at other times we expect to have to infer the answer from the substitute behavior of the client as he attempts to answer (or evade) the question. Sometimes we ask what the Inner Child needs right now; at other times we are trying to find out the client's perception of what he needed at a particular moment or period in his childhood.

Regardless of the context or timing of the question, **the purpose of asking what the Inner Child needs is always the same: to help establish, reestablish or reinforce the client's ability to pay attention to his own needs and to initiate doing something effective about them — the healthy cycle.**

More often than not, the Adult Child in treatment will not be able to give a direct answer to the question of what his Inner Child needs; in the early stages of treatment, the question may not even be meaningful to him. In order to begin to get an answer, we use a variety of information that becomes available in the process of therapy.

The following areas of information can be compared to the parts of the map that we get to look at. Close examination of them allows us to see the signs that will help us determine where we are and what we need to do to get where we want to go.

- The client's current behavior, including the presenting problem and any substitute behaviors

- Historical data about the client
- Historical origins of current emotions
- The result of using behavioral prescriptions to test the client's ability to accomplish certain tasks comfortably
- The therapist's intuitive response to the client

Current Behavior, Presenting Problem And Substitute Behaviors

When a client begins therapy, he describes the problems he is trying unsuccessfully to solve. In so doing, he usually reveals some patterns of substitute behavior. When we identify these substitute behaviors and confront the discounting that supports them, we often obtain information about the current and archaic (ie., unmet developmental) needs of the Inner Child.

In addition to the data we get from talking with the client, we use information from a questionnaire that specifically addresses developmental issues (see Appendix I for the questionnaire). By combining the information from the questionnaire with the information about the client's presenting problem, we can get a fairly detailed picture of the pattern of substitute behaviors.

Each developmental stage has a characteristic pattern of problems and substitute behaviors, which we describe below. No single item is a perfectly reliable diagnostic sign of a particular stage. When we begin to see the client's unique pattern, we can use the information to inquire in more depth about the client's history and experience at a particular developmental stage.

The following lists show some of the detailed signs we encounter in the behavior the client presents. When several signs from a particular stage are present, we explore for further information about what was happening to the client when he was that age. If additional information verifies that a problem existed at that developmental stage, we create a treatment plan to meet those needs of the Inner Child. (Information on treatment techniques is presented in Chapters 10, 11, 13, 14, 16 and 17.)

Bonding Stage

Typical Adult Child problems and substitute behaviors that may arise from the *Bonding Stage* of development are:

- Not recognizing signs of physical needs — hunger, thirst, elimination, temperature control, rest, etc.
- Not doing anything about one's physical needs
- Addictive and compulsive behaviors
- Not asking directly for anything
- Feeling desperate when a relationship ends
- Needing continuous external affirmation of one's existence
- Believing oneself to be basically unworthy — a shame-based self-definition
- Terror of abandonment
- A deep, basic lack of trust
- Frozen feelings

Exploratory Stage

Typical Adult Child problems and substitute behaviors that may arise from the *Exploratory Stage* of development are:

- Not knowing what one wants
- Being afraid to try new things
- Deferring to others' suggestions
- Feeling that someone else's suggestion is an order that must be obeyed
- Fearing abandonment and/or engulfment

Separation Stage

Typical Adult Child problems and substitute behaviors that may arise from the *Separation Stage* of development are:

- Difficulty with boundaries, with distinguishing between his own wants, needs and feelings and those of other people
- Not feeling separate or independent
- Tending to form symbiotic bonds with others
- Willingness to "do anything" to avoid direct conflict
- Not saying *no* to others directly, but often refusing to do what others want in a variety of indirect, manipulative and passive ways
- Openly and inappropriately rebellious behavior

Socialization Stage

Typical Adult Child problems and substitute behaviors that may arise from the *Socialization Stage* of development are:

- Unawareness of the possibility of asking questions, relying instead on guesses and unchecked assumptions, which are treated as if they are actual information
- Having incorrect or missing labels for feelings — anger is often labelled as sadness, or fear is experienced as anger, etc.
- Belief that incongruity between thoughts, feelings and actions is normal — they are accustomed to it
- No attempt to clarify unclear, confusing or incongruent communication, usually blame themselves if they respond incorrectly
- Belief that thoughts, wishes or feelings can lead to direct behavioral consequences
- Attempt to control their own and others' thoughts and feelings
- A grandiose sense of their own magical powers, eg., "I am responsible for (someone else's) behavior," or "If I say or do exactly the right thing, I can stop his drinking."
- Refusal to acknowledge grief, with an unwillingness to let go of something that is not working or that is gone; an insistence on clinging to a magical hope for a positive outcome

Latency Stage

Typical Adult Child problems and substitute behaviors that may arise from the *Latency Stage* of development are:

- A belief that one should know how to do things perfectly, without instruction
- A belief that every task should be done to their extremely high standards — "If I don't know I can do it well, I won't try it."
- Lack of information on organizing time for complicated tasks
- Procrastination instead of clear decision to do or not do a task
- Lack of understanding one's own reasons for beliefs and values

- Inability, ignorance and fear about negotiation; either giving in completely or insisting on having things one's own way; solutions to disagreements either win-lose (competitive) or lose-lose (mutually unsatisfactory)

Adolescent Stage

Typical Adult Child problems and substitute behaviors that may arise from the *Adolescent Stage* of development are:

- Desperate seeking of companionship to fulfill the gaps they perceive in themselves
- Refusal to accept ordinary standards of behavior
- Flaunting of differences, eg., extremes of dress
- Either dependent on others or isolated from them
- Forming Co-dependent symbiotic relationships in which they lose their sense of identity

When dysfunctional patterns are learned at any stage, they interfere with attempts to learn other healthy patterns during later years. **The younger the child was when the family dysfunction began to influence him, the more profound will be the negative effect on subsequent developmental stages.**

When corrective parenting is completed for a particular developmental stage, problems from unmet needs at other stages become apparent. When this occurs, we again ask, "How old is the Inner Child," and make a new treatment plan for the next stage to work on.

Historical Data

Information about birth order, age and number of siblings and age of client when family changes occurred, eg., change of caretakers, divorce, moves, deaths, family financial problems, schools, etc., are all helpful. Although many Adult Children don't remember specific information about childhood, this data may be available from other family members.

Historical and biographical information can help the therapist and client make "educated guesses" about how the Inner Child of a particular age might have been treated when the family was under stress. Matching these guesses with knowledge of what parenting a child needs at the age when the stress occurred provides clues to what the Inner Child may still need. (For more detailed information on how life history impacts script decisions, read Berne, *What Do You Say After You Say Hello* and Steiner, *Scripts People Live.*)

Origins Of Current Emotions

Adult Children often experience very strong emotional reactions to seemingly minor events. Feelings are triggered that appear to be out of proportion to the significance of the stimulus.

Flo's eight-year-old daughter came home late from school, saying that the teacher had kept her in detention to complete an unfinished assignment. Flo was enraged, and called the school to accuse the teacher of "humiliating" her daughter.

She was still angry several days later, when she discussed the incident in her therapy. Flo discovered that the angry feelings were familiar to her, and she remembered an incident in her own childhood in which *she* was publicly shamed and humiliated by a teacher. What angered her the most, however, was that her parents completely discounted her when she tried to tell them about it.

When the emotional reactions appear to be a "spontaneous automatic age regression", it is useful to ask the Adult Child: "How old do you feel right now?" There is likely to be a fairly specific answer, indicating that the Inner Child of that age probably needs some kind of attention and healing.

If the spontaneous age regression does not occur, as with Flo, the same information can often be obtained by asking the client, "When have you felt that way (the strong emotion) in the past?" Asking additional leading questions can uncover the needs of the Inner Child, such as:

1. "When did you feel that way in college? In high school? In grade school? When you were very little?"
2. "What was happening the *earliest* time you felt that way?"

The rich and stimulating emotional environment of a treatment group often stirs up buried emotions in the client with "frozen feelings" or emotional amnesia. As a result, these clients eventually learn to tune into the subtle messages coming from the Inner Child.

Response To Behavioral Prescriptions

Prescribing "normal" behavior, ie., things that anyone who had a healthy experience at a particular age can easily do, often highlights the developmental deficits of the Inner Child. Roxy's response to being asked to imagine nurturing herself as an infant demonstrates how quickly we can learn how a person was cared for as a child.

When we ask an Adult Child to do other simple tasks, such as asking for something (a box of tissues, a ride home, a hug), saying *no* (I don't want to answer your question) or asking questions, feelings and memories begin to surface, and we again get clues to the needs of the Inner Child.

Most Adult Children automatically treat their own Inner Child the way they were treated (or mistreated) when they were children. Examining this automatic process can reveal information about the needs of the Inner Child.

Therapist's Intuitive Response

People who have some familiarity with children occasionally feel like they are talking to a young child when they are in conversation with another adult. The speech patterns or thinking patterns or emotions of the person may be very childlike, or we may simply have the intuition that the Inner Child of a particular age is showing through. Asking a client, "Do you feel about X years old?" often brings an affirmative response. Exploring further may help clarify both what the client is responding to in the current situation and what the Inner Child needs.

General Treatment Considerations

The Adult Child's healing process includes several distinct but overlapping tasks: recognizing how the Inner Child was wounded, feeling the pain that has been buried and re-associating it to the trauma and losses in childhood, giving up the hope that the original childhood can be "fixed", and finally, using whatever resources are currently available to fill in the gaps and learn the skills necessary to be a healthy functional grown-up.

Clients rarely present their developmental issues in an orderly fashion. It is the therapist's job to organize the information he or she gets from the client into some kind of systematic form that permits mutually agreeable interventions to take place. This helps both client and therapist identify what is needed and what to do about it.

To use this information effectively:

1. Start with what the client presents. Adult Children do not usually present themselves for therapy by complaining that they are "Adult Children of Dysfunctional Families". They present a range of symptoms, conflicted life situations, struggles and pains, and they are looking for relief of their distress. *We* may understand that their problems are a result of unmet developmental needs, but it is important to begin with the client's definition of the problem. Let the client tell his story.

2. In response to the presented problem, define with the client the desired goal for change, what she wants to accomplish for herself in the therapy. Knowing which developmental stage is likely to be the source of the problem helps the therapist suggest appropriate goals to the client. It is especially useful to define such goals in terms of overt behavior, although goals about thinking and feeling differently are certainly important.

3. Discuss what prevents the client from having the goal already, what she sees as the obstacles to achieving it. It is particularly important here to focus on what the client needs to change about her own behavior in order to reach the goal.

4. Define missing or difficult behaviors as normal responses to an abnormal situation, so that the client can see that learning skills that have not been learned because of the unmet developmental needs as a valid treatment goal. The client should understand the connection between these unmet needs and the new behaviors he must practice to get the results he wants from therapy.

5. Prescribe specific behaviors the client can carry out in order to have the experience of meeting those developmental needs.

6. Together decide on the appropriate setting to test those behaviors. Some clients need more protection than others when risking change. Decide how the client will

    negotiate for appropriate responses to the new behavior.

7. Monitor progress by both feedback from the client and behavioral observation in the treatment setting. For example, does the client say *no* to the therapist when she doesn't want to do what is suggested?

8. Remember that the treatment process is more like putting together a jigsaw puzzle than following a linear path to a logial conclusion. In putting together a puzzle, you begin with the pieces that look like they go together. Most people work first with one group of pieces, then another, shifting the clusters around until they begin to fit together. What is important is that order is created out of chaos; the picture emerges.

There is no "right" way to do this. Work with any cluster — any developmental stage where the client has current energy. The order doesn't matter much. Keep at it until the picture is complete.

Corrective parenting is a treatment method that supports all parts of the Adult Child's healing process, but focuses primarily on helping the Inner Child to fill in the gaps that were created by unmet developmental needs. Once therapist and client understand what was missed, they can work together to create a plan to provide the transactions and experiences necessary for healing.

CHAPTER 10

Bonding Stage

Lou is a successful business owner, but he does everything himself, rather than ask his employees. He is frightened of being by himself at night, frequently awakening from a nightmare of being alone, small and in danger. To manage the fear, he clings to an addictive relationship, drinks excessively and has affairs when the woman he lives with is out of town.

At birth, the primary developmental task of the infant is to form a strong symbiotic bond with another human being; this is usually, but not necessarily, the biological mother. From this bonded position the infant can then proceed with the tasks of separating, individuating and becoming an independent and autonomous person.

As we worked with Lou, it became clear that he had never bonded successfully with anyone. Much of his energy was devoted to trying to bond with any available woman, so that he could avoid the terrifying feelings of isolation and abandonment experienced by his Inner Child. He tried to feel autonomous and independent by using alcohol and sex excessively, and denied that these were problems for him. He came to therapy only because his life partner threatened to leave him, stimulating his terror of potential abandonment.

115

Healthy Development

The original, healthy symbiotic bond is established, in transaction with a primary caretaker, by a repetitive process: the infant experiences some discomfort or disequilibrium, cries, and the caretaker responds in a nurturing, appropriate way, providing food, physical contact, eye contact, loving looks, etc. This mirroring exchange — the infant expressing his needs and getting a response to his own actions — becomes the prototype experience for asking for what he wants and needs throughout his life. At this stage, healthy parental responsiveness to the baby's needs and demands helps the baby establish the basic sense of trust in self and others, a sense that the world is a safe and responsive place.

Dysfunctional Development

In a dysfunctional family, the nurturing response to the infant's demands may be unreliable. As a result, the infant may learn that his attempts to get what he needs can have unpredictable results: a loving response, no response, an angry, rejecting response or even abuse. When responses are unpredictable, trust does not develop, and healthy symbiotic bonds may never be established. **Because the infant experiences that the world is part of himself, mistreatment leads him to feel that there is something wrong with *him*.** His very existence is experienced in a way that lays the foundation for deep feelings of shame.

In *Lou's* infancy, an ill older sibling captured most of his family's attention. In addition, Lou's room was far from the rest of the house, and *his* cries for attention often brought no response. The terror he felt then was appropriate to his situation, but no one was available to respond to it. The world did not seem safe because no response was available.

When *Janie* was an infant, her mother would alternate between clinging to her for her own (Mother's) comfort and rejecting her in order to meet the demands of her drunken, enraged husband. Janie believes she was sexually abused by her father in her infancy. She entered treatment because she had great difficulty establishing her independence from her mother. Even though she is a responsible professional woman, she still feared that her mother

would disapprove and abandon her to great danger if she didn't
act compliant and subservient in all situations.

Susan's Co-dependent mother tried to abort the pregnancy with
Susan, became quite ill and blamed her illness on the infant. She
angrily provided minimal care for Susan, but was completely
insensitive to the infant's expressions of needs. Susan was force-
fed food and information by her father, who was probably
psychotic; we heard tapes that he made of trying to teach her
spelling when she was 18 months old, repeating and spelling
words to her so rapidly that even an adult couldn't follow it.

In reaction to the pain of such negative responses, a baby can
learn several primitive defensive strategies: she can shut off
awareness of her needs and feelings, she can stop making
demands to get her needs met and she can learn to wait passively
for any caretaking. Later, if she does feel or express needs, she is
likely to feel ashamed of having them. The resulting pattern of
passivity is likely to be reinforced later on by family communication rules like "Don't Feel", "Don't rock the boat", or "Don't be
selfish".

Results Of Dysfunctional Development

Severe problems at the Bonding Stage of development can lead
to psychosis. More moderate difficulties lead to a deep sense of
shame and to significant passivity and discounting regarding one's
own needs. **Compulsions and addictions often develop as
substitutes for feeling the terror and rage of the desperate Inner
Child.**

Lou learned to control his fear of abandonment by compul-
sively using alcohol and sex.

Janie never asked anyone for anything for herself. She got some
of what she needed by being pleasant and by staying alert for
opportunities to serve others, who would then "be nice" to her.

Susan became bulimic; she weighed over 300 pounds when
she started treatment. She was unaware of many internal physical
sensations and signals: she could not identify hunger, didn't know
when she needed rest and could not recognize pain unless it was
severe enough to be incapacitating. She had many medical
problems, and a deep sense of unworthiness. She would wait
around after each session, clinging dependently and hoping for
extra nurturing, until we told her it was time for her to leave.

The Adult Child who had problems at the Bonding Stage usually does not experience or believe that the world is a safe place, or that relationships can be reliable. He believes that the world is unresponsive, at best, and possibly dangerous; he feels that it is shameful for him to need or want anything. He certainly cannot expect to get needs met by asking others for anything. The very idea of asking arouses shame and anxiety.

Lou wouldn't ask his personal secretary to do ordinary tasks for him. He expected her to "do her job" without clearly defining it, and if she failed to know intuitively that he needed something, he would use his valuable executive time to take care of it himself. Then, overworked and angry, he would "relieve the stress of work" by going out and drinking.

Janie felt ashamed of herself if she needed anything. She received very few strokes from anyone and didn't recognize the acknowledgment she did get; she felt depressed most of the time.

Susan would leave long, rambling messages on our answering machine about the terrible predicaments she was in, but wouldn't ask us to return her call, or even leave her phone number.

Treatment Implications

The basic treatment strategy is to help the Adult Child relearn the healthy cycle of asking for what he needs and getting a satisfying response from his environment. We provide a protected environment (as described in Chapter 7) in which he can desensitize the fear of making any demands on others by practicing asking for small, insignificant things. In the group setting, people can ask others to give them physical strokes (back rubs or other forms of massage), to sit close, to read to them, to be served coffee, etc.

This may be a difficult step. **Few Adult Children with problems from the Bonding Stage have had much experience in making direct requests. Most are used to hinting about what they want and hoping that someone will respond. Asking directly raises the fear that the past negative responses will be repeated.**

Some clients will immediately recognize the logic of practicing the new behavior of asking for what they want, and will simply go ahead and do it, even though they are uncomfortable. Other clients may have to do quite a bit more work to overcome the terrors of the past, even though they know intellectually that the group situation is safe. Often the "work" involves remembering, feeling and expressing the deep residual rage at earlier abusive treatment. (Working with this rage is discussed in Chapter 12.)

In a group setting, we often use a playful "contract" to help a reluctant but ready Adult Child take responsibility for practicing new behaviors. The client agrees to set a kitchen timer for 15 minutes, during which time he must produce the behavior we have agreed on — in this case, asking someone to do something for him. He resets the timer for another 15 minutes as soon as he has completed the task. If he does not do the task, the timer will ring, which is a signal for him to have some kind of playful consequence (eg., having Nerf Balls thrown at him) before he can reset the timer and start over.

Sometimes clients stop themselves from asking for things by concentrating on how awful it would be if they were turned down. Some of the threat may be alleviated by pointing out to the client that, if his request is refused (at least, in this setting), he will be no worse off than he was before he asked.

Because other group members are instructed to tell the truth about their responses, getting turned down is a real possibility. The client who is supposed to be asking has the opportunity to ask again, until someone does respond favorably. We may confront the client's reluctance by asking what he does when a store is out of something he wants. Usually he recognizes that he would simply search for it in other stores until he finds it.

Adult Children who didn't form healthy symbiotic bonds in infancy need support in order to experience that their most basic needs are okay, and that their very existence is not shameful. One way of providing that support is with direct verbal affirmations. In *Becoming The Way We Are,* Pamela Levin suggests some affirmative statements that can be said directly to the Adult Child or that he can say or write to himself. There are specific sets of statements for each developmental stage.

Levin's "Affirmations for Being", ie., the set of statements relevant to the Bonding Stage, are ideas that normally would be conveyed, both verbally and nonverbally, to a newborn infant. In a healthy environment the infant who is received joyfully learns:

- "You have a right to be here."
- "Your needs are okay with me."
- "I'm glad you're a (boy, girl)."
- "You don't have to hurry, you can take your time."
- "I like to hold you, to be near you and to touch you."

Because the infant Inner Child is preverbal, words alone are not sufficient to convey these messages. In the safe environment of the group, we suggest some specific activities that help the Inner Child incorporate these new beliefs and reestablish an inner sense of trust and acceptance.

- Get held and touched gently and nonsexually by someone who feels good about it and enjoys doing it.
- Let yourself be carried.
- Permit someone to feed you.
- Get a full-body massage.
- Wear a blindfold and let someone lead you around for a few minutes.
- Soak in a hot bath and gently rub your whole body with soap or lotion.

Many of these activities can be carried out in the group treatment setting, with the therapist providing or supervising the nurturing parenting. It is important for there to be sufficient agreement and protection for this kind of activity. Nobody (including the therapist) is *ever* pressured or forced to participate in these activities.

The Search For Unconditional Love

Adult Children who didn't bond successfully often spend their lives searching for unconditional love, and find Co-dependent relationships instead. **It is the birthright of an infant to receive loving attention without having to meet any expectations or conditions.** Disturbances in bonding occur when parents expect and demand certain behaviors from their babies.

Adults in our culture do not have the rights and privileges of babies. We must meet basic social expectations before others want to share loving relationships with us. Healthy grown-up love is conditional, unlike the love between a parent and an infant that is unconditional.

The Adult Child, living in a grown-up body, while sometimes feeling like an infant, is caught in a dilemma: how to get the unconditional loving support he needs to learn to nurture and accept himself, while still meeting the social requirements of being a grown-up.

Regressive Treatment: Parenting The Inner Child

Corrective parenting can help solve this dilemma. Corrective parenting, in its purest form, is the process in which the therapist directly "parents" the exposed Inner Child of the client. This is done contractually, ie., with explicit verbal agreement, when both the therapist and the client agree that the client's Inner Child needs a particular type of parental response in order to learn a skill or resolve a problem. The therapist agrees to provide the response, while the client agrees to behave like a child of a particular age and to be as open as possible to receiving the parenting and learning from it.

There is an agreement that the therapist will not parent the client *in general,* but only the Inner Child. Even then, the parenting is only done at a specific time and place, usually during the group session. It is clear to both client and therapist that the main purpose is to help the client learn to nurture his own Inner Child by experiencing and incorporating the nurturing that was missed. The Parent and Adult Ego States of the client are available to observe the process; in this way, the client can eventually learn how to provide self-nurturing. Corrective parenting is appropriate when it becomes clear that the client does not have sufficient internal resources to provide self-nurturing at a particular developmental stage.

Once the client and therapist agree to the procedure, the client is instructed to focus his attention on the infant Inner Child, and to allow the more grown-up parts of himself to withdraw and merely observe. He is gently told to relax, that he doesn't have to do anything and that he can just "be". The therapist or other "parent" holds him in his arms as if he were a baby, strokes him gently and sometimes says the affirmations listed earlier, for the benefit of the observing Ego States. (See p. 122.)

Either of us is capable of and willing to nurture either male or female clients. When we have asked our clients about this, we have learned that sometimes it is important to the client who does the holding, and sometimes it isn't. Sooner or later, every client who needs to do this primitive level of work seems to need to do it with both a mother and a father figure; the client always gets to choose.

In the group setting, clients often decide to do this "regressive" work after they have observed others doing it and have recognized the need in themselves. When a client decides that he is ready, he is instructed to focus on his own physical sensations, to move or make noise (cry) if he is uncomfortable and not to pay any attention to the needs of the therapist. The therapist is responsible for taking care of himself, rather than expecting the regressed client to accommodate to his comfort. The therapist will ask others for physical assistance in moving the client, if necessary.

This position can be varied to suit the comfort of the "infant" and the "parent."

The therapist responds to the expressed needs of the client, shifting physical position, attending to temperature control with blankets, etc., as he would with a baby of chronological age. He makes eye contact and noises if the client is alert and interactive.

Often, before the client "gets little", ie., enters the regressed state, there will be an agreement to provide a baby bottle of milk, water or fruit juice when he lets us know he is ready for it.

Once the client is used to the process, we may change the procedure to a more "natural" sequence. Instead of having one of us hold him while he regresses, the client lies down somewhere in the group room and gets into the regressed state by himself. Once in the state, he allows himself to cry to be picked up, stroked, fed, etc., according to his own internal experience of his needs. Many important issues get worked through as the client deals with the necessity of demanding, in the regressed state, that we respond to his needs.

While taking care of the regressed client, the therapist may have conversations with other clients who are present in group, just as a parent caring for an infant of chronological age would do.

This procedure continues for the agreed-upon length of time; it is ended when the therapist tells the client, "It's time to grow up, now." Often the client is somewhat reluctant to resume grown-up functioning immediately, so 10 or 15 minutes are allowed for this "growing up" process. It is important that the client be capable of adult functioning before leaving the therapy setting; we ask, "Are you old enough to drive?"

The entire process is explained in detail to the client before we make the agreement to do it. Depending on the needs of the client, the process may be repeated in each session for a period of weeks or months. Both therapist and client sense the completion of this phase of work when basic trust is established.

For example, Pat writes, "Things started changing when I started to feel some kinship with the other members of group, and when Laurie suggested I do 'baby work'. Week after week, month after month all I did in group was 'baby work'. It was then necessary for me to discover how to take care of the 'baby within' at home, too. Sometimes I called for reassurance. Slowly at first and then with increased momentum, I started enjoying the child within. My self-talk changed. My outlook changed. The way I related and felt about myself and others changed, and so much more."

Regressive work is extremely powerful and is likely to activate strong feelings and memories. Some clients are threatened or repulsed at the idea of work in this form. We assure them that nobody is expected or required to do their therapy work in this form, and that many people complete their therapy without ever "getting little". We invite people who have strong reactions to seeing this work to examine why it is having such an impact. This self-examination helps clients recognize their own archaic issues that have been activated by seeing someone else's work. We then discuss how the reactive client will deal with those issues.

We do the regressive work in a group setting, for the protection of everyone involved. By its nature, the work brings the therapist and client in very close physical contact. Both client and therapist need complete protection from any hint of destructive sexual contact. Therefore, the work must be done *openly.*

A therapist who is learning to provide corrective parenting should solicit and use feedback from clients, supervisors and consultants. There are many techniques that can best be learned in an apprentice or workshop setting. Common sense, a knowledge of appropriate parenting and respect for all concerned are essential.

CHAPTER 11

EXPLORATORY STAGE

Fay is a devoted wife and mother, and her husband's business partner. She flirts openly with a business associate, and her husband becomes angry and privately asks her to change her behavior. She gets furious at him for not letting her have fun, not letting her do what she wants.

When we carefully examine Fay's desire to do what she wants to do, we discover that she has never in her life felt the freedom to pursue her own interests. She has spent most of her life trying to please others, a strategy she learned when she was beaten by her alcoholic parents for showing any initiative of her own. She is now in a benign environment, but her Inner Child is convinced that it is unsafe to ever do what she wants. She unconsciously invites others to restrict her, because she is so afraid of the consequences of actually following her own initiative. When she succeeds in getting the restriction and disapproval, she takes it as proof of her belief.

Healthy Development

Between nine and eighteen months of age, the growing child's developmental task is to begin the process of becoming a separate, autonomous person. This is typically accomplished by gradually moving away from the primary bond (usually with the mother) in order to learn about the environment through active exploration. The healthy child takes vigorous initiative to scan and search her world; she creeps, crawls, toddles, walks and runs away from her secure attachment to the parent, so that she can investigate her environment.

The exploring child actively searches the environment for interesting people, sights, objects, sounds and kinesthetic experiences. As much as possible, she needs freedom to move herself around physically, to go after those things that attract her. A beautiful, detailed description of this process can be found in *Oneness and Separateness: From Infant to Individual,* by Louise Kaplan.

The exploratory child needs caretakers who are visible, available and responsive to her coming and going. When the child approaches the parent(s), they respond warmly; when the child moves away to other things that interest her, the parents permit and encourage this, while still remaining available to her. They provide protection by making sure the environment is safe, such as "babyproofing" the house, and by gently distracting the baby if she approaches an unsafe situation or gets into something she could damage.

Ten-month-old **Geri** crawls around the island in the middle of the kitchen. For a few moments, she cannot see mother working at the counter. When she emerges around the far corner and can see mother again, she crows in excitement. Mother turns to her and smiles, says warmly, "Hi, Honey, you found me," and then turns back to her work. Geri picks up a toy and starts to examine it.

This kind of healthy parenting supports, affirms and reinforces the baby's natural ability to go after what she wants. This is the psychological foundation for knowing what we want and for taking initiative to get it.

The exploratory stage can be frustrating to both parent and toddler. If the child has any freedom of movement at all, the parent must be on constant alert to prevent her getting into something dangerous. The child may climb on and off a lap six times in five minutes. She may then be into the dog food, the kitchen cabinet and the tool box within the next few minutes. Caring for an exploring baby can be exhausting, and the primary caretaker needs periodic relief and support.

Dysfunctional Development

In a dysfunctional family, it may be very difficult for the parent to provide the healthy combination of responsiveness, freedom and safety that an active exploratory child needs. Because the child pushes for her own needs, the parent may see the situation as a constant battle. The parent may react to the resulting frustration in a variety of ways that interfere with the baby's healthy development.

One of the most frequent unhealthy parenting patterns is to confine, restrict and isolate the child excessively, in order to avoid having to handle the difficulty of constantly keeping track of her.

Jack was tied into his crib at night and was kept in a playpen until he was three. When he got agile enough to climb out, his father built a lid on it. As an adult, he usually acted in an extremely polite and controlled manner, although he occasionally punched holes in walls when he thought anyone was trying to control him. He reacted to his fear of being engulfed by covering it with furious anger.

Bonnie's mother was proud that *Bonnie* had never touched anything she shouldn't. She had left all of her beautiful bric-a-brac out and carefully watched Bonnie when she first began to explore. Each time Bonnie reached for something, Mother shouted *no* and slapped her hand. It only took a week or two to train Bonnie to "be good". As an adult, Bonnie was very timid and terrified of doing anything that would displease anyone.

Lou was placed in a well-protected playroom, far from the household activities, so that he wouldn't disturb anyone. He had lots of toys but almost no human contact for hours at a time. As an adult, he feared being alone and demanded constant attention from a series of lovers.

A parent who is emotionally needy herself may see the baby as a source of gratification; the focus of the parenting becomes the parent's needs, rather than the child's. As a result, the child may experience being overwhelmed and engulfed by the parent's needs, but will be unable to move away in her own direction because of the threat of abandonment. She may become a "good child", setting the stage for later becoming "The Responsible One".

Janie was constantly hugged, cuddled and fussed over by her Co-dependent mother, who felt insulted and confused when Janie tried to turn away from her. This behavior took place whenever they were alone, but when father was drunk, mother put Janie in a room far away where she could play (and cry for attention) without disturbing him and arousing his anger.

As an adult, Janie was terrified of doing anything mother would disapprove of, and furious at mother for trying to control her life. She was also afraid of getting too close to her husband, because he might restrict her as mother did. She distanced him by immersing herself in her work. She never played or did anything just for fun, and concentrated on trying to meet all her responsibilities and obligations.

Another unbalanced pattern is for the parent to regularly distract the toddler from her natural course, thus taking away the initiative from the baby. Distracting a child from a dangerous situation is appropriate; **providing continuous stimulation that keeps the toddler from exploring freely, however, teaches her to ignore her own exploratory impulses.** Instead of exploring on her own, she learns to respond primarily to the external stimulation and stroking provided by the parent. This **over-parenting, which centers around getting the child to adapt to the parent's agenda, interferes with the child's natural awareness and expressiveness, and eventually can teach her to manipulate for strokes by trying to please others.** The constantly distracted child may develop the substitute behavior of constantly seeking high levels of stimulation — when what is really needed is the freedom to get in touch with her own internal motivation and needs.

Emily, a 38-year-old divorced actress, came to treatment because of the intense depression she experienced when she went home after a performance. She would get very excited and stimulated as long as she received applause, and crashed as soon as she was alone.

The focus of Emily's life is on looking good: impeccable clothes, stylish entertaining and impressive partners. She participated in a series of unsatisfying addictive relationships, trying to get powerful but self-centered men to provide continuous affirmation and applause.

Emily was the oldest child in an alcoholic family. Her mother gave up trying to be close to her authoritative alcoholic husband, and devoted her life to her children. Emily had almost continuous suffocating attention and pressure to perform; she decided at an early age that performing was the only way she could get her needs met.

When Fay, Bonnie, Jack, Lou and Janie are asked, "What do you want for yourself?" they usually reply, "I don't know what I want." Emily wants (and gets) lots of things, but they somehow never satisfy her.

Results Of Dysfunctional Development

The Adult Child with problems from this stage typically doesn't take initiative to identify and act on his own needs, interests and desires. We have discussed a variety of reasons for this pattern: learned passivity, fears of abandonment or engulfment, the desire to please whomever he perceives to be the parent(s) in any situation.

The work of the Exploratory Stage marks the beginning of the baby's inexorable progress toward individuation and separation from the primary parents. Many Adult children whose problems originated in this stage have great difficulty understanding and experiencing their own boundaries when they are with others. They lose their sense of themselves in unhealthy symbiotic relationships with other adults. When they seek therapy, they are often diagnosed as having Borderline Personality Disorder.

Treatment Implications

Treatment is designed to reestablish the suppressed exploratory drive, so that the Adult Child can become aware of what he wants and can learn to take action to get it.

Knowing what he wants is often difficult for an Adult Child, who was systematically trained to ignore what he wanted — often in favor of what others wanted. We work to reestablish the natural pattern of recognizing a desire and doing something active to attain it.

Most Adult Children have occasional impulses of wanting something when they notice someone else with it, or are stimulated by an advertisement. However, they usually dismiss these thoughts quickly and forget the impulse. To capture these fleeting awarenesses, we ask a client to create a wish list or an "I want" list. He agrees to always carry paper and pencil. Every time he notices wanting something, he writes it down, instead of letting it slip his mind. He then agrees to take action to get some items on the wish list, and to report what he has done so that we can acknowledge him for it.

Sample situations follow:

Fay wanted time to read. She started to take off several hours a week to do so.

Janie wanted to take a vacation. She brought travel brochures to group.

Lou wanted to learn to play the guitar. He had never even held one, so he went to music stores, told sales people he was a novice and held twelve different instruments in about two weeks. He eventually took lessons.

Jack wanted to use his physical strength. He spent a day helping construct a playground for neighborhood children.

It doesn't matter whether the item is large or small; the important thing for the Adult Child to learn to do is to notice the want and to initiate some action that is motivated by wanting it.

In the group setting, we encourage our clients to take initiative to explore and experiment, and offer positive acknowledgment when they do so. We invite them to pay close attention to their own impulses, however slight, to explore and examine any and all physical aspects of the group situation (the colors of the pillows, the texture of the rug, the toys in the closet, etc.). They make a specific agreement to act on these impulses and actually explore what attracts them.

Joan grew up in a family where everything that was not required was forbidden. She reported that she had no idea of what to do when all her planned tasks were accomplished. She constructed rigid schedules for herself to avoid this problem.

When she started the assignment of exploring in group, she sat very quietly for about 20 minutes. Then she walked over and examined a variety of items on the window sill. She found copies of Levin's developmental affirmations, read them and brought them to show the therapist. She identified the Exploratory Stage affirmations as statements that were completely foreign to her experience:

- "You can get attention or approval and still act the way you really feel."
- "You can do things and get support at the same time."
- "It's okay to explore and to experiment."
- "It's okay for you to initiate."
- "You can be curious and intuitive."

These developmental affirmations are useful for anyone with problems originating at the Exploratory Stage. A toddler normally learns them through response to his self-initiated activities.

Joan decided that her homework would be to think about how to use these permissions in her daily life. In the next group session, she took out and examined many toys and began to play with some of them, inviting another client to play with her. In the following session, she reported allowing herself 30 minutes of free time every day to use according to her impulse of the moment.

Sometimes our clients have trouble actually trying some exploratory tasks. When this occurs, the kitchen timer intervention, described in Chapter 10, can be useful. They agree to explore something new before the timer rings.

An effective way of dealing with the fears of abandonment and/ or engulfment in this stage is to set up a situation that simulates the natural process of coming and going that would occupy a healthy exploratory child. In group, we encourage the client to move freely around the room, particularly focusing on moving toward and away from the therapist (parent figure). He is given strokes (if he wants them) when he is close, and is waved at and acknowledged when he is on the other side of the room.

When *Connie* decided to practice this, she sat next to me *(Jon)* and asked me to put my arm around her. She stayed in one position for about 20 minutes. When questioned, she said that she was afraid to leave because someone would take her spot and I wouldn't let her come back. I told her to tell me when she wanted to come back and that I would find a place for her near me. She went to participate in another conversation, did several other things and then did ask for and receive more stroking from me.

Many clients will not ask for what they want (especially physical strokes) because they perceive that the therapist is "busy" with someone else. They "take care" of the therapist the way they took care of their parents, by not making demands or requests. We tell them to ask anyhow, as a healthy child would, and let *us* take responsibility for figuring out how to respond to their needs.

Outside of the group setting, there are a number of behaviors that the client can practice in order to simulate exploratory behavior. A typical "homework" assignment might be to walk slowly through a large department store, picking up things that seem attractive, feeling them and looking at them closely, then putting them down again and moving on to the next interesting thing. Driving different routes to familiar places, eating messy food with fingers, eating new foods, or focusing specifically on the texture, flavor, colors, etc., of familiar foods, can all be exploratory activities. One client developed a fascination with extreme close-up photography when he was working on this issue.

Regressive Treatment: Parenting The Inner Child

Direct corrective parenting of the Adult Child in the regressed state is also useful. An exploratory baby should not need to consider whether or not the object she is reaching for is safe or appropriate or approved; she should just go ahead and reach. When a client recognizes that she needs the experience of exploring without having to inhibit or control herself, we suggest that she energize her six-to-eighteen-month-old Inner Child and do whatever interests her, letting us provide the appropriate protection. If the client agrees to work this way, we give her more specific information and instructions before proceeding.

We instruct the client to use only the physical movements appropriate to a baby: creeping, crawling and occasionally walking. We either take out age-appropriate toys or let the client do so before she gets little. The toys are scattered throughout the room. We remind the client that babies explore people as well as objects, and give permission to approach and explore anyone or anything that seems interesting, and to leave when they are no longer interested. Language usage is limited to single words; clients are instructed to make distressed sounds if they need anything they can't get for themselves. Clients are asked to remove timepieces, so that their observing Adult and Parent Ego States do not take over and limit them. At the end of the allotted time, *we* tell the client that it's time to grow up.

The needs of the Exploratory Stage are in addition to, not instead of, those of the Bonding Stage. A client doing regressive exploratory work, therefore, will still probably need holding, nurturing and possibly feeding. We ask if they will want a bottle and what they want in it (milk, juice or water), and offer it when they seem distressed. In this stage, the client may feel like holding the bottle and feeding himself.

It is the therapist's responsibility to protect an age-regressed client. We make sure that dangerous and/or fragile objects are removed from the room. If the regressed client gets something she shouldn't, we distract her and offer a safe replacement (babies are easily distracted). We always make sure someone — one of us, or an assistant — is aware of what the "baby" is doing.

We make frequent eye contact with the baby, wave and play Peek-a-Boo. We stroke him physically when he comes within range, and allow him to move on when he wants to. Later, we may grab him when he comes by, playing "I've Got You Trapped" or "You'll Never Get Away" — games that real toddlers find so delightful.

When a client first starts to do this work, we are careful to offer very little structure, direction or stimulation. The client has already learned to adapt herself to outside stimulation; the purpose of this work is for her to rediscover her own motivation (energy for moving). We try to stay out of her way. Sometimes a regressed client will spend a long time huddled in a corner doing nothing. When someone doesn't tell her what she should be doing, she doesn't (at first) know what to do at all. There is a great temptation to try to amuse her, but we discourage it. Later, when she is in her Adult again, we will tell her that it is probably better for her to sit there doing nothing, and wait until she becomes aware of her own desires, than to have anyone reinforce the problem by giving her something to react to.

Susan had been doing this work for several months, and had become fairly energetic about seeking stimulation. When making her contract to be about 14 months old, she said, "You can start the No-No's now." She had incorporated the idea that babies should be disciplined — harshly. She felt she had experienced all the nurturing she was entitled to, and was ready to deal with the punishing restrictions she was sure would follow. The concept of just being protected was a shock and a relief. Susan is gradually learning that taking action to get what she needs is satisfying and safe.

Regressive work can reactivate many intense feelings that were suppressed in infancy. Becoming aware of and working through those feelings is crucial for the Inner Child's healing process. (In the next Chapter, "Working With Feelings" — Part 2, we discuss this process in depth.)

CHAPTER 12

WORKING WITH FEELINGS — PART 2

Roxy is flat on her back on a mat in the center of the group room, screaming, kicking and thrashing; eight people are restraining her carefully, but firmly, so that she can move her body, but can't hurt herself or anyone else.

After spending several months in group, reluctantly following our recommendation to practice asking for strokes and noticing what she wants, Roxy has begun to recognize that she has felt angry all her life. She sees that the anger is within her, and that it is not being caused by her external circumstances. She sees how she has been using her current circumstances to justify venting some of the anger, usually in an inappropriate or destructive way. Her Inner Child fears that she will destroy "everything" and will be abandoned if she expresses the rage she really feels.

Even though she is terrified, she has asked for the protection of the group, so that she can release her controls and feel and express these powerful, primitive feelings.

Once Roxy discharges these feelings, she feels vulnerable and helpless, like an infant, and is held and nurtured. Later, her Inner Child fears that she has done something wrong, bad and dangerous, and that she may get hurt or be abandoned. She is directed to pay attention to the difference between how she is actually being treated now and how she would have been treated as a child. She accepts the reassurance that she is now safe.

The kind of anger that Roxy is expressing is the primitive rage of an infant whose needs are not being met. Although these kinds of feelings may be an issue for many Adult Children, infancy is not the only source of anger, nor is restrained rage work the only way to deal with it. Several different kinds of anger are characteristic of Adult Children; the therapist's job is to help the client learn to identify and differentiate between them, and to learn what to do about them.

Some clients know when they are angry. They may report frequent angry episodes, usually where they blame someone else for their unhappiness. This kind of anger is often a substitute for other feelings. Working with these clients usually involves helping them learn how they create the situations that justify the angry feelings.

Barry talks about how angry he is that his wife rejects him when he reaches for her to cuddle with him in the morning. When questioned about the larger situation, he sees that he waits to reach for her until the moment she is ready to get out of bed and start her day. He justifies waiting by telling himself that doing something sooner would be intruding on her privacy. More importantly, we discover that he only reaches for her after an extended time of feeling deprived of contact and not saying or doing anything about it.

Some clients intellectualize anger, but don't feel it. They may only suspect that they are angry, reporting feelings and sensations that must be interpreted to them as indications of anger. Clients with "frozen feelings" may report on situations (perhaps of abuse) very calmly, without feelings, and the therapists and other clients feel angry. Sometimes these clients avoid their feelings because they fear, "If I allowed myself to feel, I would destroy the room, or I would want to kill someone."

For example:

Wanda: *I think I'd like to deal with my anger at my mother.*
Therapist: *That sounds like a good idea.*

W: *But I don't really feel anything.* (She calmly describes being locked in a dark garage and beaten by her mother. She was told [by the mother] that her attempts to escape the beating only made Mother angrier.)

T: *Close your eyes and pay attention to the sensations in your body; tell me what you feel.*

W: *It really hurts down here* [in her upper abdomen].

T: *There's a word or a sound in that place. Can you let it out?*

W: (starts to cry): *Get away from me! Stop that!*

With support and encouragement, Wanda goes on to feel and express some of the anger from that situation, by continuing to say the things to her mother that she didn't dare say aloud when she was a child. She feels relieved and surprised afterwards, and recognizes that she has a lot more to do.

Different Types Of Anger

There are distinctions between different types of anger that are useful for helping the client and therapist decide what to do.

Current Anger

Current anger is usually related to a present situation that the person wants to change. (If the person doesn't want to change anything, we are probably dealing with a substitute feeling, and need to find out what is underneath the anger.) Current anger is directed at another person who is doing or not doing something that interferes with the person getting what he needs or wants. The client can be helped to problem-solve about how to accomplish the outcome he wants (see Chapter 8).

Old Anger

Old anger is the anger people feel when they remember past incidents of unfair, cruel or inappropriate treatment by another person. It is similar to current anger, but is directed at someone who is not present or available, so that no actual problem-solving can be accomplished by expressing the anger.

This kind of anger does need to be released, however, and can usually be resolved by feeling and expressing it to a fantasy image of the perpetrator.

Self-Centered Anger

Self-centered anger is directed at common expectations and limits (and at the people who represent or communicate those limits). It is characterized by resisting or objecting to ordinary rules, eg., traffic lights and speed limits, and by feeling controlled and intruded on by someone who expects some ordinary consideration. The person is angry at having to take other people's needs and wants into account. Self-centered anger can be directed at either current or past situations and people.

Self-centered anger usually reflects an unmet need to separate or individuate, and will be discussed in detail in Chapter 13.

Rage

Rage is primitive, global, diffuse and nonverbal; it is undirected anger that arises from significant mistreatment during infancy. It can be present at the same time as the other kinds of anger, and can even be masked by them.

Rage is distinctly different from the other types of anger, in that it is not aimed at anyone or anything specific. It comes from a much earlier stage of development than the other types, a time when the infant cannot distinguish between self and others. It is a primitive expression of the feeling that something is terribly wrong. The Adult Child often experiences rage the way an infant does, throughout the whole body. When clients become aware of this feeling, they are usually very frightened that it could destroy them or others. It is usually kept under tight control, and the client needs adequate protection to discharge the feelings safely.

Each type of anger requires a different set of responses from the therapist. In order to find out what we are dealing with, we ask several specific questions.

"What Are You Angry About?"

A description of a particular person or incident, either current or in the past, usually indicates current, old or self-centered anger. "I'm angry at myself" rules out self-centered anger, but always masks some other type of anger or some other feeling.

Self-centered anger can sometimes be recognized in the answer to this question by its abstract quality; it is directed at "The System", or "Them", or "Our Society". Even if his anger is directed at a specific individual, the self-centered person often sounds as if he would rather stay angry than solve the problem.

If the answer is "I don't know," we ask about the circumstances that may have stimulated the feelings. If the client says things like, "I've always felt this way," or "I experience tension in my body most of the time," or "It doesn't feel like it's about anything," we suspect that rage is present.

"When Have You Felt This Way Before?"

This question is asked when the client has described a current situation, but we suspect that there may be more going on. Often the client will respond by identifying a particular past situation. In that case, it is necessary to work separately with both the current anger and the old anger in order to completely resolve the issue.

An answer like "Whenever someone gets in my way like that," suggests self-centered anger. "I can't remember *not* feeling this way," suggests that rage may be present.

In general, a client with current anger needs to learn to express it in a problem-solving way (see Chapters 8 and 9). Old anger and rage need to be expressed and released in specific ways discussed below. Self-centered anger can only be resolved by giving it up (see Chapter 13, "The Separation Stage").

Avoidance Of Anger

Expressing angry feelings, especially if they involve rage, can be a painful and frightening process, and it is understandable that many people try to avoid this difficult work. One of the most common methods Adult Children use to avoid dealing with anger is to declare that they understand their parents did the best job they could, and that they now forgive their parents and are ready to move on. This position is a worthwhile goal, but **true forgiveness is only achieved by working through the angry feelings, not by denying and suppressing them.**

In therapy, the old angry feelings will surface. (If they don't, something is missing in the therapy.) When this happens, the Adult Child's most likely reaction will be to try to suppress the feelings again. If he succeeds, the original problem of discounting the Child's feelings is repeated. This time, however, the Adult Child can be confronted with the information that he is treating his own Inner Child the same way he was treated originally.

Calling it "Child Abuse" is a dramatic — and effective — way to confront this issue.

We remind clients, "Feelings are a signal that you need something. Turning off your feelings doesn't get you what you need; it just puts you in the position of continuing to discount your own needs."

A further confrontation is to point out that discounting themselves opens the door to a variety of self-limiting, self-defeating and self-destructive behavior patterns:

1. Playing psychological games that justify feeling the ever-present anger by blaming it on someone else (see *Games People Play* by Eric Berne)
2. Acting out unpredictably the ever-present angry feelings when controls are weakened by the use of chemicals or by external stress
3. Feeling intense shame and worthlessness, with a resulting impairment in the capacity for intimacy
4. Extending the strategy of discounting to everyday problems that only get worse when they are not attended to
5. Creating internal physiological stress that can lead to stress-related illnesses ranging from headaches to cancer
6. Having insensitivity to the subtle feelings that can be used to guide our important life decisions
7. Lacking spontaneity and joy

Unresolved angry feelings from past mistreatment must be felt, expressed and released, if the Inner Child is to be healed and to learn appropriate self-nurturing. Discharging the angry feelings does not, in itself, automatically cure all of these problems. Grief work is also necessary before the losses of childhood in a dysfunctional family can be worked through (see Chapter 15, "Working With Feelings" — Part 3). In addition, new healthy ways of handling anger must be learned, in order to avoid re-creating the old patterns.

Most Adult Children are reluctant to express the angry feelings, even in the relatively safe situation of therapy. They know what happened in the family if someone got angry. They may remember the scenes, as in the example of working with Wanda, or their bodies may remember by cringing and wanting to run when they hear raised or angry-sounding voices. They fear being physically or emotionally hurt or abandoned if they express their feelings.

Learning To Release Anger

We often find it useful to help our clients become desensitized to relatively mild expressions of anger before they are ready to work through the more intense feelings.

Sarah is so afraid of attracting negative attention that she speaks almost too softly to be heard; we repeatedly remind her to speak up. Once she is willing to do that consistently, we teach her how to make angry noises. With her chin thrust forward, her shoulders back and her chest out, she is to make loud, guttural and growling sounds. She practices the physical posture in group, but insists that she must practice the noise-making privately. After a week of practice at home, she demonstrates her new skill in group and receives much applause.

In *Larry's* extended family, disapproval was expressed by shunning the offender, excluding him from any contact with other family members. He was reluctant to acknowledge aloud his angry feelings, for fear of being abandoned. He was, however, willing to make somewhat abstract lists of things he was angry about. He eventually progressed to writing and then reading aloud (but not mailing) angry letters to his parents.

When Adult Children have reasonable current relationships with their aging parents, they fear that getting in touch with the old anger and rage would disrupt these relationships. They may claim that they are not angry at their parents now (which may be true or may be defensive).

Most of the Adult Child's anger at parents, even in a current situation, is actually aimed at the 20-to-30-year-old parents who mistreated him thirty or forty years ago. This old anger needs to be expressed, but expressing it to the real parents is potentially destructive. We tell clients, "The parent you need to work this out with is the one you carry around in your head; *that's* the one you need to express your anger to." (If there is a current problem, we help them look at the problem-solving methods described in Chapter 7, "The Treatment Environment" and Chapter 8, "Working With Feelings" — Part 1.)

We rarely suggest that people confront others directly with old anger. The other person is often unavailable, physically or psychologically, to hear it. Even with current anger, the direct expression of it may create more problems than it solves. Anger that is inappropriate or impossible to express directly to the actual target can be resolved by expressing it to an *image* of the other person.

To help clients with the process of releasing anger (not rage, which will be discussed later), we suggest that they imagine the person they are talking about is present. We then ask them to talk directly to that person, and say, with feeling, the things they want to say. We make it clear we are helping them to release the feelings in the safety of the therapy, not recommending that they express the feelings directly to the other person. For example:

1. "Tell your boss how you feel about the way he passed you over for promotion."
2. "Tell your [dead] father the things you always wanted to say to him."

We usually ask the client to report on the imaginary person's responses; sometimes we invite the client to take the role of the other person and carry on a dialogue. In either case, we monitor the process closely to keep the client focused on the direct expression of the feelings. Regardless of the specific technique used, opening the door to old feelings often releases a flood of emotion, as years of unexpressed anger, grief and fear come pouring out.

Magda is aware of angry feelings toward her self-centered lover, but is unaware of her general feelings of rage at being abused and neglected when she was tiny. I suggest that she imagine her lover is there in the therapy room, sitting on a pillow in front of her, and that she tell him how she feels. She begins in a polite, ladylike manner to apologize to him for her anger. I remind her that this is a safe place to tell the truth about her feelings. She begins to sound angry. As the anger builds, I ask her to push down on the pillow. Finally she pounds the pillow with her fists, shouting her feelings until she stops, exhausted. She pants, "There's more — I feel like I'm going to explode!"

Rage Work

Magda is now aware of her need to express the primitive rage she has stored and layered over with other feelings since her abuse in infancy. Magda, Roxy and others who gain access to these primitive levels of the Inner Child need a safe method for discharging both the rage and the primal fear of expressing it. They handled the danger of expressing the rage and terror they felt in infancy by splitting off these feelings. Now, as the feelings come flooding back, the Inner Child must be reassured that she will not be annihilated for daring to communicate the pain. The protection needed for expressing this primitive rage is much more extensive than what is needed to express current or old anger.

The first level of protection for doing rage work is to insist that it be done contractually. Although we may confront a client with our observation that he probably needs to do rage, we make it clear that we expect the client to take responsibility for telling us when he is choosing to do the work. It is possible, but difficult and potentially dangerous, to handle a spontaneous outburst of rage. Our experience is that people who need to do this work *can* manage to contain it until enough protection is available, and we insist that they do so.

We provide psychological reassurance to the Inner Child by giving the client nurturing messages specifically intended to counter the fears we know are there:

1. "What you are feeling is only *part* of yourself; it's not all there is to you, and it's not all there is to the world."
2. "It's not dangerous here; you're afraid because you're remembering another time when it *was* dangerous."
3. "You've seen other people do this, and nothing bad happened to them."
4. "We are here to take care of you now, and we'll still be here when you're through; we won't go away because you're mad."
5. "You're safe; no one here is going to hurt you, and no one who isn't here knows that you're doing this."
6. "You won't explode or disappear, and neither will anyone else; we won't let you hurt anybody."
7. "You don't have to take care of anyone by hiding how you feel."

Holding For A Restrained Rage

We provide physical safety by restraining the client on a thick foam rubber pad in the center of the group room, thus taking control of the amount of the client's physical movement. The client must be able to move, but must be protected so that she cannot hurt herself or anyone else. Without some physical protection, clients fear that their rage is so destructive that they can never risk releasing their own controls. They experience great relief when they discover they are physically unable to do any damage.

Doing a "rage hold" safely and easily requires eight or nine holders: one person for the head, one for each shoulder, hand and leg and one or two to hold the feet. That way no single holder has more than he can handle, and even very large or strong people can be protected by smaller ones.

When we give the instructions for the holders, we make a point of having the client hear what we are saying. We want her to have the information that the first priority of the situation is her support, protection and safety. The general instructions for the holders:

- Remove all jewelry, glasses, pens, belt buckles and any other potentially damaging objects.
- Never put any pressure directly on a joint.
- Ask for help if you need it.
- If you have feelings, let them come; you can hold and cry at the same time. It's okay to be scared; tell someone if you are.
- If you don't want to be a holder, then don't do it.

In a new group, all rage hold tasks and positions, described below, are carefully demonstrated. An experienced group shows new holders what to do.

The client lies on his back on the mat, a sixty-by-eighty-by-four-inch foam slab. The head is held, usually by the therapist, by placing one or both hands, palm down, on the forehead. No pressure is applied unless the client tries to raise his head from the mat, and then only enough to keep the head from coming up.

The person restraining a shoulder lies on her stomach at a 90-degree angle to the client. The holder slides her "foot-side" arm, palm down, under the armpit and places her other elbow next to the client's ear. She bends that "head-side" arm down across the nearest collarbone and just inside the point of the shoulder, to provide the restraint against the shoulder coming up off the mat. The hand of the holder's foot-side arm grasps the bicep of her own head-side arm, holding it firmly down on the mat. The client's arm sticks out from under the armpit of the holder's foot-side arm. (See below.)

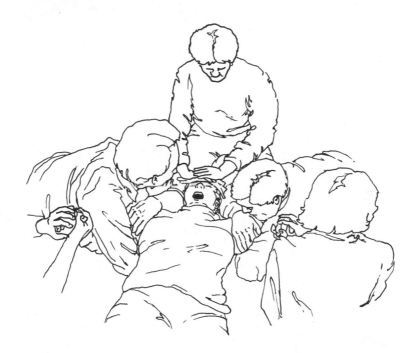

The right hand is restrained by locking thumbs with the holder's right hand, palms facing each other. A soft foam ball is placed in the client's fist, between his fingers and the back of the holder's hand, so that he cannot hurt himself or the holder with his fingernails. The holder's other hand goes over the client's knuckles to control, but not prevent, movement; the object is to keep anybody from getting hit. The wrist is never held. The left hand is held in the same manner, but reversed. (See top of p. 146.)

Legs are restrained by putting weight on the lower thigh, just above the knee. The holders can face either the client's head or feet. Lying on her side at a 90-degree angle to the client's leg, the holder places her bottom arm over the top of the lower thigh, between the legs and then under the leg. The holder then rests the weight of her upper body on the leg just *above* the knee. The object is for the client to have to carry the weight of the holder's body as he tries to move his leg. (See bottom of p. 146.)

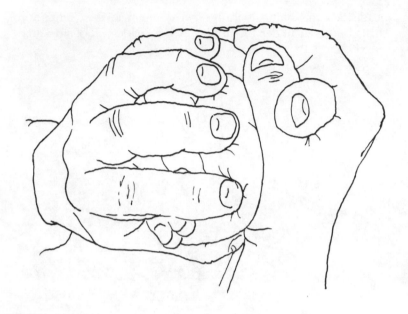

Feet are held only to prevent the client from getting leverage by bracing them on the mat. The holder sits facing the client's head and puts his hands under the ankles, just above the heel. If the client attempts to dig in his heels or put his feet flat on the mat, the holder simply pulls the foot toward her. (See below.)

After the holders are in place, the client is invited to test the restraints, to see that they are secure and comfortable. If necessary, we make adjustments.

When everything is ready, we tell the client, "You can do whatever you need to do. We'll take care of you. We won't let you hurt yourself or anyone else. We'll stay with you. You're safe."

When the client feels safe enough, he lets the rage erupt, screaming (sounds, not words), and thrashing until the physical energy is spent. The amount of energy released can be truly amazing; moving like an enraged infant, the client uses every part of his body to discharge the energy. Sometimes the energy comes in waves. This work seldom goes on for more than 10 to 20 minutes; it is too physically draining.

If the client has trouble releasing the controls, we encourage him to breathe deeply into his abdomen and to make sounds with every exhalation. We continue the verbal reassurances. Sometimes having him shout *no!* or *help!* can help him open the door to the preverbal material. Sometimes, even with all the protection and encouragement, the client still isn't ready to release the controls. When that happens, we stroke him for going as far as he did, and reassure him that he didn't fail, that this isn't a performance and that he can do it when he is ready.

Some clients prefer to do rage work without being restrained; this preference may come from an internal sense of what they need, or it may come from terror of being held down. In either case, we have them lie in the center of the mat and surround them, at the edges of the mat, with large pillows. The pillows protect the client from thrashing himself off the mat, and protect the bystanders from getting accidentally hit. This form of rage work can be done in an individual session, if necessary.

Immediately after doing the rage work, many clients want to be held and stroked. If we feel that they are in an age-regressed state, we may offer them a baby bottle of water or milk, so that the infant Inner Child can experience being nurtured even though they get angry. Whether they are regressed or not, they often need reassurance that they really did what they did, that what they did was okay, that nobody is angry at them and that they won't be abandoned.

Some people, as children, constructed the belief or fantasy that the enraged part of them was something abnormal or inhuman. To counter these beliefs we often say, "I heard how angry you are, I know you're not an animal, you're just an angry little boy (girl). It's okay to be angry, and to let people know you're angry, if you're being hurt or not getting what you need."

Follow-Up

We always do this work early in a two-hour group session, so that the client has enough time to rest and regain adult functioning afterward. When his Adult is more available, we tell him that he may be hoarse and sore for the next few days because of the physical exertion. We also tell him that, because he broke a lot of internal Parent rules by doing this work, his Inner Child may feel scared and vulnerable, and may even try to deny that he really did the work. We tell him he can call us if this happens, so that we can reassure him again, if necessary. We also invite him to ask other clients who have done similar work for ongoing contact and support. Often several rage release sessions are necessary for a client to clear out the archaic feelings.

Clients who witness this work and have repressed their own primitive rage and terror are often frightened and need reassurance and protection while the rage work is occurring. The therapist should be alert for this and carefully explain to new clients what is going to happen, how the holding is protection and not punishment and whom they can go to for reassurance during the work. An assistant or experienced client should be alerted to provide any needed assistance. If the upset clients are properly supported during and after another's rage work, they can see that discharge of rage is possible and safe, and they become less fearful of expressing their own feelings in the future.

chapter 13

SEPARATION STAGE

Morton, an Adult Child, is a very timid man, constantly apologizing for minor or imagined faults, and always "trying" to please others. He readily agrees to every assignment the therapist suggests, but the assignments somehow never get done. Morton never says *no* to the therapist's suggestions, but the outcome is the same as if he had. The therapist feels as if she is dealing with a stubborn two-year-old who is hiding out in the disguise of compliance.

An important developmental task for a two-year-old is to establish a sense of independent identity, without sacrificing closeness to the parents. A new kind of closeness to the parents must be developed, one that respects the separate identities of both the parents and the child. Morton never established this independent identity.

Healthy Development

In this Separation Stage of development, which lasts from about eighteen months to about three years, the child learns that his parents (and the rest of the world) are not part of himself. He learns that they won't always do exactly what he wants done, and that he, in turn, doesn't always want to please them. In the process of this learning, the child forms his basic behavioral patterns for coping with the fact that what he wants and what others want do not always match. Ideally, he learns that *thinking* is the best solution to this fundamental conflict.

There are two distinct phases to this learning process. In the first phase, the child "experiments" with being separate by being oppositional to whatever the parent wants. The experiment is necessary because the child has no previous experience with what it would be like to be a separate person. The closest he can come to being *separate* is to be *different.* The experiment can be thought of as a test to see if it is safe to want something different than what the parent wants.

After the child has gathered enough data from the experiment (ie., has been stubborn, willful, rebellious and obstinate for several months), the parent reaches a point of extreme frustration. Fortunately, at about the same time, the child begins to signal, by his behavior, that he is ready for more responsibility. The next phase begins when the parent starts to insist that the child take into account (think about) what the parent wants *as well as* what the child wants.

When **Gerry** starts to exhibit rebellious, oppositional behavior, his parents respond with patient good humor. When he doesn't want his food, they remove it; when he wants it back a few seconds later, they return it — and take it away again a few minutes later when he begins throwing it on the floor. When he starts to cry, they take him out of the high chair and let him roam around the kitchen and find his toys. When they need to take him to the babysitter, they allow plenty of time for him to assert himself while getting him dressed. They set firm limits only in areas involving safety and remain flexible in as many other areas as possible. In addition, they support each other in the frustrating task of parenting their two-year-old.

After several months of this pattern, the parents notice that Gerry is interested in some new behaviors: putting toys in a box, looking for, finding and bringing things, learning to use the potty chair, etc. All of these new behaviors require some degree of thinking, remembering and problem-solving. At first, he does these new behaviors only sporadically, then with increasing consistency.

The parents gradually begin to expect Gerry to do the new behaviors regularly. He usually complies, but sometimes gets very stubborn about refusing. It often looks as if he is challenging his parents, trying to find an answer to the question, "What will you do if I don't do what you want me to?" By this time, there is no longer any doubt about whether or not Gerry *understands* what they want him to do, or whether he *knows how* to do it. He clearly has the information, but he is now testing the limits.

They finally start to insist that Gerry use the information that they all know he has. They tell him, "You can't come out of your room until you put away the toys (all three of them)." He pretends not to know what they are talking about, and tries to come out. They firmly send him back, telling him that he knows how to get to come out. He sulks for 20 minutes, finally picks up the toys, announces what he has done and comes out proud and smiling. He decides for himself to do what is expected. He isn't forced. He gets what he wants by doing what his parents want — but not until he is ready.

This sequence is repeated over and over again, about different issues. In this phase, the healthy parent resists the common impulse to tell the child repeatedly what he already knows (ie., what the parent wants him to do and how to do it). In this way, the parent conveys the expectation that she expects the child use his own information to solve the problem. This strategy puts the child in a bind: he wants to do something about being uncomfortable with the parent's insistence, but he can only do so by letting go of the safe and familiar symbiotic pattern of having the parent think for him and control him. After a struggle, the child decides that it is to his own advantage to use the information, ie., to think for himself. The parent approves of this decision, and both win. This process gradually breaks the symbiosis and convinces Gerry that he is a separate and capable little person.

In Transactional Analysis terms, the Child decides to use his own Adult to solve the problem of being unhappy about the parent's expectation. He decides to think about his feelings and what to do about them. **This decision is a critical prototype for later healthy functioning; it is a decision to use one's own internal resources for problem-solving, rather than relying on those of others.** Children raised in dysfunctional families rarely accomplish this task.

Dysfunctional Development

The child from a dysfunctional family often tries to be "good" at this stage, and thus avoids the oppositional behavior essential for healthy individuation. He may have been traumatized by earlier feelings of abandonment, and is trying not to attract negative attention. He may be "good" because he learned a pattern of adapting to the expectations of others in the Exploratory Stage.

The child who is "good" is often too involved with earning approval (or avoiding disapproval) from parents even to attempt to become separate. It never occurs to her to attempt any opposition. Clients often recall being told what good babies they were, that they never went through the "Terrible Two's". Whatever the reason for being "good", the child remains symbiotically attached to the parent.

These children do, of course, get toilet trained and learn to take responsibility, but they do so only in order to please the grown-ups, rather than as an expression of their own growing maturity. They rarely experience their own strength and autonomy.

Jane was the oldest of nine children. By the time she was two, she had two younger siblings, and her mother had no time to cope with any of Jane's attempts to be autonomous. She never learned to say *no*. She did learn to adapt to exaggerated expectations of maturity; for example, at the age of 11, she meekly complied with orders to drive her six siblings 30 miles, although she had never before driven a car.

Jane was referred for treatment because she had become extremely fearful of leaving her home; she wouldn't answer the phone unless it was a coded ring from her husband. She explained that each time she ventured out into the world, people would ask her to do things. She would agree to do them without counting her needs at all, and would quickly get overwhelmed by trying to meet everyone's expectations. (Jane is a good example of the "Super-Responsible" person described by Janet Woititz in *Adult Children of Alcoholics.*) The only alternative she could think of was to hide.

Results Of Dysfunctional Development

Children who do not complete the separation process are likely to grow up to feel, as adults, that they must always be attached to another individual in order to feel safe and complete. In intimate relationships, they try to please, abandon their power to the other and easily slip into Co-dependence. They may alternate between clinging to a partner for nurturing and angrily pushing the partner away when he fails the impossible task of nurturing perfectly. This pattern is typical of the Adult Child with a *Borderline Personality Disorder.*

Ruth expects her husband to make all the arrangements for their vacation. When the accommodations aren't to her liking, she berates him for being irresponsible and tells us she hates him "because he never cares about what I like."

Such a person may behave overtly in a "super-responsible" manner, while covertly longing to be "taken care of" in an infantile way. When pressure becomes too great, she may collapse into illness or other incapacitation (become "Super-Irresponsible"), abandoning all responsibility in an attempt to get the caretaking she needs.

Jan raised seven children almost single-handedly while her husband was an active alcoholic. Although she took on most family responsibilities, she firmly believed that she wouldn't know what to do without him. When he entered a treatment program and stopped drinking, he started making all the decisions for the family and for her. She meekly carried out his wishes, and became so dependent on him that she "couldn't manage" to shop alone or cook without his help. She would often get headaches and he would have to come home and take care of her.

Colleen, an Adult Child, took on greater and greater responsibilities at work. Just before a major project was due for completion, she decided she was just too nervous to continue, locked her desk, left the office without telling anyone and never returned. Her employer tried to find out if she was ill and called her home. Her sister answered and said that Colleen was just too upset to come back — ever. While cleaning up the mess she left behind, the employer discovered that many of the responsibilities that Colleen had accepted had been literally stuffed into the back of drawers and left unfinished.

If the child in a dysfunctional family does become oppositional, the parents may be too distracted by their own problems to provide the appropriate responses that he needs. When parents provide no limits or expectations, for example, the child, who should be learning to take others into account, remains in the position that "the world revolves around me". As an adult, the person may experience a great deal of the self-centered anger described in Chapter 12, and may show the super-irresponsible pattern of behavior.

The Peter Pan Syndrome, by Dan Kiley, and *Men Who Hate Women And The Women Who Love Them,* by Susan Forward, both describe men who operate from this self-centered position. Although the pattern is not exclusively masculine, men who remain in that position receive far more social acceptance and "understanding" than women. Men with this pattern usually do not come for treatment, unless they are being pressured by their partners; they are often diagnosed as *Narcissistic Personality Disorder.*

Ken, a successful professional, was the "Crown Prince" in his family, allowed to do whatever he wished. In his "committed" Co-dependent relationship, he is now insisting on his right to take a vacation with another woman. After all, he says, he needs his freedom. He is incensed that his partner, who supported him through his divorce and other bad times, is "trying to control him" by saying that she will leave him if he goes on the trip with the other woman. He is currently seeing his third competent therapist in as many years; he left the previous ones, saying that each was too controlling.

When the dysfunctional parent responds to the child's rebellious behavior by getting upset, he/she may overpower the child with total restriction and repression; the child learns that what he needs doesn't count at all in the face of what others feel. This is a way to learn to be super-responsible. He may be furiously angry at this discounting of his needs, but the anger is controlled and hidden; it is likely to show up in adulthood as a passive-aggressive pattern.

At two, **Adele** was beaten with a switch when she tried to get her own way. At eight, she was beaten severely for wanting the same privileges as her brother. When she stubbornly refused to cry, her enraged father continued the beatings and became even more restrictive. She finally decided to "be good".

Adele holds a very responsible job, but she married an alcoholic who berated her verbally and then abandoned her. She feels deeply ashamed of herself whenever she becomes aware of her own needs, and is beginning to realize how much anger she has suppressed.

Both kinds of inappropriate parenting, overrestrictive and overpermissive, are often present in a pattern that is unpredictable to the child. He learns to count only himself at certain times, only others at other times, but never both self and others at the same time. This accounts for the difficulty in intimate relationships, where both self and other must be taken into account.

Robert is the oldest of five siblings. He was indulged by his mother, but severely repressed by his angry alcoholic father, who left the family when Robert was seven. Robert became the man of the family and tried to take care of everyone; but he would occasionally have temper tantrums like his father, when his siblings got out of line.

Robert's wife left him, because he alternated his benevolent indulgent behavior with increasingly violent outbursts. He berated her for not focusing all her attention on him "after all he'd done for her". In therapy, he occasionally breaks through his angry denial to the hurt little boy who can't figure out how to be himself and get close to anyone.

When the early symbiotic attachment is not broken effectively, the child doesn't make the decision to think about his feelings. Consequently, he can't learn to think and feel at the same time. He functions as if there is a barrier between his Child Ego State (feeling) and his Adult Ego State (thinking). (See Chapter 4 for a description of the transactional patterns that are produced as a result.)

The Adult Child with this developmental problem does not find out that his Adult, his ability to think, is a tool to help him resolve the problems that arise when he and others want different things. He can only see such differences as meaning that there is a contest between what he wants and what others want. Depending on his specific programming and experiences, he may believe that his role is to be the loser in such contests, or that he is supposed to be the winner and that others are supposed to lose. The possibility of both "winning", ie., both people getting what they need, does not occur to him.

Treatment Implications

The Adult Child who has never experienced the rebellion that leads to establishment of an independent identity must be helped to realize and experience her own independence. In counseling adults with this pattern, it is common to teach them "assertiveness", and focus on their being more demanding of what they want. We see this as a limited approach, which tends to reinforce the "You *or* Me" position that is the source of the problem. We prefer helping people learn to focus on "You *and* Me" and to negotiate for what they want.

In working with clients who focus excessively on "You", we do not expect them to move immediately from that position to the "You and Me" position. Most will first go through a "Me *instead of* You" phase, which helps them break up the old patterns of thought and behavior. This phase may be a problem for the client's family and associates, who may lose their privileged status, but it does serve to raise the consciousness of those associates who were unaware of the client's sacrifices and accepted them as their due. In most cases, the "Me instead of You" phase is relatively short, if the therapy concentrates on cooperation rather than competition.

Marilyn, who came to treatment because of depression, is gradually learning to take herself into account. She is letting her family know that she is no longer everybody's servant. She took a job that fascinated her, even though her husband disapproved because it didn't pay as much as he expected her to earn.

Marilyn is one of the former "good children", whose unwillingness to refuse others' requests led directly to the depleted state she was in when she started treatment.

To engage this type of client in the treatment process, we comment, "It sounds like there are very few things you say *no* to," or "It sounds like you are always saying *yes*." After the client has agreed that reluctance to say *no* is a problem, we proceed with the following treatment plan:

- Saying *no* in private
- Saying *no* semipublicly
- Saying *no* publicly and meaning it

Step One

During this step, the client gains practice in saying *no* aloud, in private. We often suggest, as a homework assignment, that she say *no* 20 times a day, including variations such as, "I don't want to," and "I won't." When she is at home alone, she is to say *no* about everything she doesn't want to do:

- "No, I don't want to get out of bed."
- "No, I don't want to clean up."

- "No, I don't want to call the repairman."
- "No, I don't want to go to work."
- "No, I don't want to stop for the red light."
- "No, I don't want to drive in this traffic."
- "No, I don't want to do what I am supposed to do."

We especially encourage the client to say *no* to things she knows she needs to do and has been procrastinating about. During this step, we tell her to continue to actually do the things she ordinarily does.

This mechanical procedure helps the client begin to experience the natural rebelliousness of a two-year-old who is beginning to engage in a separation process. It gives the client permission to overtly acknowledge feelings she has been attempting to suppress. It is also relatively "safe", because she can do it in complete privacy — it involves no transactions with anyone else.

When a client is in group, we ask her to agree to say *no* or *"I don't want to"* loudly and at random, and not necessarily in response to what is going on in the group. This agreement produces behavior that would be considered rude in other settings, but which is supported in group, as a way to practice getting in touch with the energy of the rebellious Inner Child.

Frank recognized the need to practice saying *no* in group, agreed to do so and then sat silently through the rest of the group. Our first response was to recognize and stroke the covert rebelliousness by saying, "I guess you are acting out the *no* instead of saying it." Then we explained to Frank that hiding his rebelliousness brought the same results as if he had refused to do the task in the first place, except that his *Rebellious Child* doesn't get any direct support, recognition, permission or strokes for his behavior.

We explained again that the idea is to own and integrate the rebellious part, and that doing so requires him to make his rebellion public, in a safe situation. We suggested the timer contract, and he, like most clients who finally acknowledge covert rebellion, agreed to use the timer and accept a consequence if he failed to say *no* aloud. His whole face lit up when he finally did start to say *no*; he loved doing it.

Step Two

After the client has had a week's practice in saying *no* in private, we encourage him to agree to say it semipublicly. He agrees to tell certain close friends and associates that he is learning about himself and wants to practice making changes. He then asks whether it would be all right with them if, for a period of time, he automatically said *no* to everything they ask him to do, for practice, and then discussed with them whether or not he was willing to do what was requested. During this stage, most clients quickly reconsider their *no* and do whatever is asked of them. In group, clients usually enjoy saying *no* when asked to do things, when they really understand that they are safe and won't be either forced to do something or abandoned.

This assignment involves more risk, because the client needs to involve others in the process. It simulates the beginning of the Separation Stage by providing benign "surrogate parents", who will merely listen to the "rebellion" without getting upset. Simultaneously, it reinforces the position of the client as a responsible adult who does not automatically enjoy the rights of a two-year-old and must contract with other grown-ups for this special treatment.

Step Three

The task here is to say *no* and mean it. We encourage the client to continue to say *no* semipublicly and consider how she feels about each request. If it is something that she strongly doesn't want to do, we encourage her to refuse to do it, and to negotiate with the person who made the request, so that either the request is handled some other way (if necessary) or both of them are satisfied even if it is not handled. The important lessons here are how to negotiate and how to count the other person's feelings and desires while maintaining her own right to refuse the request. (We will discuss negotiation in more detail in Chapter 16, "The Latency Stage".) The purpose of saying *no* at this stage is to recognize and give validity to the part of the personality that has wanted to say *no* all along and has not done so because of fear of unpleasant consequences.

This procedure encourages the client to use the rebellious energy in a healthy, grown-up way. She must acknowledge her own dislikes (often easier then discovering her likes) and think enough of herself to refuse unpleasant activities to which she used to agree automatically.

At this stage in therapy, a client sometimes decides to end treatment. Although therapy is always done with the client's agreement and consent, we are usually suspicious about a client who wants to leave at this point. Especially if the client can only give Child, rather than Adult, reasons for leaving, we see the client as trying to "prove" her autonomy without actually solving the problem.

We encourage the client to stay, pointing out that she cannot get her attempts at independence acknowledged and supported if she isn't here for it. If she leaves now, she reinforces the belief that her Inner Child will be abandoned, especially by caretakers, if she tries to be autonomous. Acting out the problem in this manner makes it very difficult for the Adult Child to learn how to be with other people whose wants are different from her own.

Nell, a recovering 23-year-old alcoholic, wanted to leave, because she didn't believe she could think differently than we did and still stay in treatment. In her family, she was ridiculed if she wanted to do anything different than her alcoholic parents. She wasn't reassured until she had a series of individual sessions, in which she cautiously experimented with sharing her own ideas about her life.

After the individual work, she was able to communicate effectively to her mother that she was no longer going to do everything mother seemed to expect her to do.

Responding To Overtly Rebellious Behavior

When the client presents overtly rebellious behavior, a different strategy is called for; but the logic of the interventions is the same, ie., meeting the developmental needs that were missed at this stage. (If the overt rebellion is still in the form of, or associated with, active chemical abuse, the following recommendations are far less effective and should wait until the client is well into the recovery process.)

The client who is overtly rebellious typically experiences such behavior as his way of asserting and insisting on his autonomy. It is useful to confront him with the fact that he would not need to spend so much energy proving his autonomy if he didn't doubt it in the first place. Furthermore, (he is told), in order to be rebellious, he has to wait to find out what someone else wants, in order to resist it, rather than taking initiative to determine what he wants from his own internal needs. He is thus being just as dependent on others as if he were complying with them.

Dan's initial treatment goal was to feel more freedom in the relationship with his girlfriend. He perceived her as "too controlling" when she complained about his repeatedly showing up several hours late. He felt that he was "just being himself" by stopping off for a few drinks with the boys on his way to see her.

When we looked more closely with him at his pattern of behavior, he discovered, to his chagrin, that the only time he bothered to "stop off for a drink with the boys" was when he had already agreed to meet his girlfriend at a specific time. He saw how he was setting himself up to believe that she was controlling, stopped the "Game" and began to examine more closely his rebellious relationship with his mother.

Once a client begins to see the validity of this point of view, he can begin to deal with the idea that his sense of autonomy is a function of his feeling that he *is* the one who makes his choices, not anyone else, and that he can't really feel autonomous when he is letting someone else's agenda steer him. This usually becomes especially vivid to him when he recognizes that he has been refusing to do some things he *wants* to do, just because someone else (including the Parent in his head) wants him to do those things. A useful intervention here is to have the client practice being aware that he is the one who chooses to do things.

Once the rebelliousness becomes conscious and deliberate, the client needs to *decide* to give it up because he *wants* to, rather than because he is complying with someone else's expectations.

One way of defining the goal of working with the Adult Child with problems from this stage is that we are trying to break down the barrier between the Child and Adult, so that the person can think about his feelings and be aware of how he feels in response to his thoughts. Levin's "Affirmations for Thinking" are useful in this process. We convey them to the client both verbally and nonverbally:

1. "I'm glad you're growing up."
2. "You can let people know when you're angry."
3. "You can think about your feelings, and you can feel about your thinking."
4. "You can think for yourself. You don't have to take care of other people by thinking for them."
5. "You don't have to be uncertain; you can be sure about what you need."

Some clients strongly resist making this difficult move toward true autonomy. Adult Children often "know" intuitively that taking this step is irrevocable. If they do it, they almost literally can't go home again. They can never again interact with their family of origin by remaining a child, by shutting down feelings and going into denial. (Even after this transformation, people report reverting to old behaviors and feelings, but they are aware of doing it and usually get out of it quickly.)

This is often the last major work our clients do before they complete treatment. They don't usually leave immediately, but stay for weeks or months to test that they can still receive affection and support even though they are independent and autonomous.

Often clients need strong support to make this decision for autonomy. The support takes the form of actively confronting their attempts to be symbiotic with us. These attempts often look as if the client has apparently forgotten much of what he learned either months ago or a few minutes ago.

Instead of teaching him again, we recognize this behavior as the equivalent of Gerry saying, "What toys?" It is an attempt to get us to think for him symbiotically, or to "take care of him" (without his asking directly for it) one more time.

We must refuse the covert invitation to be symbiotic, and turn the client back to his own resources, *if we are sure he has them.* If we are not sure, we risk reinforcing the original family situation, in which the child was left to his own devices, rather than responded to by nurturing and available adults. If we pay attention, the client will, by his behavior, let us know what he is ready for in the way of confrontation, just as the young child lets the parents know he is ready to learn to think for himself.

The confrontations of these invitations to symbiotic attachment can be simple and easy, or they can be intense and dramatic:

After a year and a half in group, where people frequently go out of the room to get a hot drink, *Jack* asks if he can be excused to get a cup of tea. We tell him he already knows the answer, and go on with other work. He looks confused, and, in a few minutes, gets up and gets what he wants.

Connie, who has done a great deal of work about how to manage confrontations with her angry husband, asks us what to do in a situation she has handled successfully in the past. We ask what she has thought of doing. She tells us and says, "I know that will work. I guess I didn't need to ask, after all."

We agree with Connie, and ask her why she invited us to think for her. In response, she begins to get in touch with how frightened her Inner Child is about the abandonment feelings being stirred up by her impending divorce.

Sam, who has made enormous positive changes in his life, comes to group in an angry funk. He says that he hates everyone and in two years has made no progress, and furthermore, "Therapy is a ripoff." We suggest that he have no interaction with anyone in the group until he is ready to tell us what the problem is.

He goes to a corner of the room and sulks for 45 minutes. He comes out crying, and tells us about how sad he is feeling about the ending of an important relationship.

Following this incident, Sam calls almost daily to tell us how stuck he is on some problem he is thinking about. We sympathize and tell him that it's okay with us for him to figure out what to do. He usually solves each problem within a few minutes. After several weeks, he reports to his group that his Parent is now telling him that he can think and solve problems, instead of saying that he is stupid and inadequate.

Regressive Treatment: Parenting The Inner Child

Direct corrective parenting of the two-year-old Inner Child is particularly useful for Adult Children who were badly abused, physically or emotionally, for assertive behavior. It is also useful for clients who have already done regressive work at earlier developmental stages.

During the first phase of the regressive work in this stage, we instruct clients to explore toys and people as they would in the Exploratory Stage, coming and going as they choose. We tell them to use simple language — words, phrases and short sentences — to communicate what they want. We suggest that they can practice being assertive about what they want and don't want, using words like "Mine", "I want", "Give me", and finally *no*.

When *Ned* started to "be Two", he was very sweet and compliant. When he went to the toy closet and started pulling out toys, we gave him our standard instruction: "You can take out whatever you want, and when it's time to go home, you will have to put away whatever you take out." He said, "okay," and when we told him to put toys away, he did so without complaint.

A few weeks later, he was more assertive. When told to put the toys away, he said, "Don't want to." We made a game out of picking up the toys, and he happily joined in and helped put them away. Each week he found more and more things to do instead of putting the toys away: he tried taking a nap, cuddling up to someone, playing a game or just being stubborn. It took more and more inventiveness to get his cooperation. Finally, he refused, providing us with a signal that he was ready for the second phase of the regressive work.

In the second phase, we make an *agreement* with the client that we will insist that he does something he doesn't want to do, and will provide consequences if he doesn't do it. We instruct him to be as stubborn and rebellious as he feels, for as long as he wants. The client agrees to limit the rebellious behavior to the group setting, and then only when he has contracted for it. The client must agree to energize his Adult before leaving the protected environment. Often we will engage in the struggle with the Child for an hour or more, and then have a rational discussion with the Adult about the progress of the work.

When Ned refused to put away the toys, we told him he could choose whether to put them away or to stand in the corner twice as long as it took someone else to put them away. He chose to stand in the corner.

The next week, he tested us still further; he started banging a heavy wooden truck into the wall — a forbidden activity. When we told him to stop, he refused. We told him he would have to stand in the corner until he agreed to follow the rules of the playroom and not damage the wall. He stood there for over an hour.

Each time we asked if he had decided to follow the rules, he angrily said *no!* He poured out all the rebellious energy he couldn't express to his abusive parents. When we had him "grow up" at the end of the group, he reported how good he felt about continuing to refuse. He contracted to come to several extra groups (at no charge) to stand in the corner and feel his own power to choose. After two weeks of this, his Inner Child agreed to obey the rules, and, amid much cheering, came out of the corner.

During the time Ned was going through this process in group, he reported that he was getting an amazing amount of work done in his business, completing projects he had been putting off for many months and getting several new contracts.

As the Adult Child gets the corrective parenting he needs, either directly or indirectly, he can release the energy he has been using to maintain a precarious balance between his need for autonomy and his need for attachment. When the work is completed, the client no longer has to go around proving that he is autonomous; nor does he have to try to get close to others by stifling his need for autonomy. He knows, deep within his being, that he is the only one who is really in charge of him, and can relax and use his energy to get on with his life. He can now use oppositional energy to resist things that are destructive to himself or others.

CHAPTER

14

SOCIALIZATION STAGE

Most Adult Children have trouble understanding how their thoughts, feelings and actions influence their lives. Growing up in dysfunctional families, where distortions of information are routine, and where the grown-ups reinforce magical beliefs, they never **learn that some things can be controlled, that most things can't be controlled and that there is a way to tell the difference.**

Nikki decided that to protect herself, she had to control her own needs and feelings and to focus on taking care of others. Like many Adult Children, she has largely forgotten most of the painful events of her childhood, and the feelings associated with those events. As I help protect another client who is expressing intense rage, I notice that Nikki is looking more and more upset. She retreats to the far corner of the room and pulls a blanket over her head. I'm relieved; she finally feels safe enough in the group situation to allow us to know how little and vulnerable she usually feels.

Leaving Jon to continue supporting the rage work, I go over to Nikki and lift a corner of her blanket. She angrily tells me, "I'm not here!" As I hug her, blanket and all, I recognize the typical response of a preschool child who believes that she can magically control her environment by stating that something is the way she wishes it is. I tell her that I can see that she is upset (implying that she really is here, despite her wishes to the contrary), and ask how old she is.

Finally, as I continue to hold her, Nikki sobs out her terror, telling us the story. She is four, coloring quietly outside her mother's closed bedroom door; Mother is "sick" again (from the effects of alcohol). Nikki believes that she caused Mother's illness by being bad, and Mother has just yelled at her again for making too much noise.

Nikki tells me how she tries to make Mother well by being good, but it just isn't working. She tells me how bad she is, certain that if she wasn't bad that Mother would be well. I explain to Nikki (ie., to her Inner Child) that she hasn't done anything wrong, that she is not bad and that not even a grown-up could make Mother be different.

To help Nikki's Inner Child experience more of what she should have had when she was four, I encourage her to play, and to ask for nurturing (holding, stroking), whenever she feels like she wants it. Nikki remains in the state of a four-year-old for a while, gets a storybook from the toy closet in the group room and asks another group member to read to her. She periodically interrupts the conversations around her with questions about other people's feelings and behaviors.

Healthy Development

In the Socialization Stage, healthy three- to five-year-olds are actively engaged in getting information about the way their world works, in order to determine where they fit within it. The newly autonomous child is busy discovering exactly what kind of person she is, what she is capable of doing in the world and what she can expect from other people.

Four-year-olds constantly ask *Why?* and are curious about everything. They experiment with provocative and nasty behavior in order to find out what happens.

In this stage, children need to learn that there are differences between thoughts, feelings and actions. They need to learn that they are not omnipotent: that their thinking things or wishing them doesn't make them happen, that magic isn't real, and that people have reasons for wanting what they want and doing what they do. They learn these things in transaction with parents and others who give them appropriate information, answer questions, set limits, correct misperceptions and provide opportunities for learning.

Four-year-olds naturally make up their own explanations of what's going on around them and act accordingly. They understand just enough about the world to get it hopelessly confused. If the distortions and misunderstandings of reality are not recognized and corrected, they will persist in the child's belief system about the world.

An alert and caring parent will respond to the child's questions, and will actively take the opportunity to correct misperceptions, even without the child asking direct questions. (Children do not necessarily distinguish between "asking" and "telling"; in fact, they often confuse the meaning of the two words.)

> **Jenny** (to her slightly older brother): *I know a girl who has a penis.*
> **David:** *You're stupid!*
> **Mom** (overhearing): *She's not stupid, she hasn't learned yet. Jenny, if a person has a penis, that makes him a boy; girls have vaginas, not penises.*

When a healthy child completes the Separation Stage, he decides to be a separate person. In the Socialization Stage, he is busy finding out what kind of person he is. Because one of the critical distinctions our culture makes between people is on the basis of their sex, this becomes a very interesting topic to children of this age. In a dysfunctional family, there will be many opportunities for the curious child to develop distorted, inaccurate and incomplete ideas about sexuality, gender, sex roles, etc.

Dysfunctional Development

Sexuality is only one of the areas in which the dysfunctional family may not support the growing child's needs for clear, accurate and understandable information. A dysfunctional parent will either not recognize the need for correct information, will not correct the misperceptions, or will actively contribute his/her own distorted attitudes, feelings or behaviors.

Dory, age 34, came to treatment because she was incapacitated by fears stimulated by her mother's death. Dory was taken to a funeral when she was four. She became upset that the person in the coffin didn't have anything to eat. Instead of explaining that dead people can't eat, her mother reassured Dory that she would remind the priest to put food in the casket. Dory's Co-dependent mother was undoubtedly uncomfortable with the difficult task of explaining death to a four-year-old. She responded to her own discomfort in a way that discounted her daughter's needs for accurate information. In fact, Dory received so much distorted and incomplete information from her mother, that, by the time she had to deal with the reality of a death, she was completely unequipped to handle it.

Children who have already been programmed to be "good" are likely to ask few questions, or, conversely, may use questions as simply another manipulation for eliciting strokes, rather than for gaining information. They rarely engage in provocative behavior. They gave up pursuing the objects they wanted in the Exploratory Stage, and now they don't pursue the information they want.

These "good children" are inhibited in expressing their view of the world. Because they do not expose their beliefs and opinions, their opportunities for corrective feedback are limited; thus they tend to hold on indefinitely to incorrect or inaccurate beliefs about who they are and how the world works. Because there may be inadequate real controls ("I won't let you hit your sister") the child learns to control herself with the exaggerated fantasies of all the awful things that might happen if she misbehaves. Some forms of religious instruction reinforce this distorted self-control.

In a dysfunctional family, these fantasies are often based on the chaos children actually observe. The ability to learn the difference between real consequences and exaggerated fantasies is impaired.

In *Janie's* family, the children would be herded into the basement to hide when their father came home drunk. As an Adult Child, she experiences terror and withdraws anytime she hears a raised voice. Her Inner Child assumes that "loud" always equals "dangerous".

In an alcoholic family, the child can rarely accomplish the developmental tasks of this stage. The natural belief in her omnipotence is reinforced instead of challenged. She concludes that she is the cause of the family's distress, and that there must be something she can do to control it. Parental statements like, "You make me sick," "You're a bad girl," "If it weren't for you, I'd be happy," and "You make me feel better," are especially confusing, because they reinforce the idea that her thoughts and feelings (which she knows are "bad"), her very existence, can make things happen in the world.

Because she is responsible (in her own mind) for the problem, the little child becomes seriously intent on the task of fixing the family — using woefully inadequate tools. She never gives up hope that, if she tries hard enough and controls herself and the world around her well enough, she will finally be able to fix things. When she inevitably fails at this impossible task, she thinks of herself as "bad".

Because of the chaos, she never learns which of her behaviors produce results, and she never gives up her belief that her thoughts and feelings must also be controlled to keep her world safe. She is usually much too busy or preoccupied to play.

At four, *Nikki* always tried to be good, but never seemed to succeed; even her turning pages quietly made too much noise for her hung-over mother. She quit asking questions because she learned if she asked questions, she was criticized for being stupid. Nikki became convinced that she was a bad girl, and that it was her fault her mother was sick.

Treatment Implications

When we treat clients with problems from the Socialization Stage, we recognize that we are dealing with adults who are thinking, feeling and often acting like four-year-olds. Each client is likely to need a great deal of information, structure, nurturing and permission. Instead of asking for these things, the client demonstrates his need for them in the same way a four-year-old does: by showing evidence of misinformation, magical thinking and inappropriate conclusions about reality.

Bea learned, as a child, that nobody paid any attention to her unless she was very upset. Now, in group, she overdramatizes her problems and exaggerates her feelings. When we tell her that she doesn't have to do this, and that she can just ask for what she wants, she looks surprised. She practices the new behavior for a while, to see if it works. A few weeks later, the hysterical behavior has disappeared.

With most Adult Children, our treatment process begins with encouraging, inviting and cajoling them to ask questions. One of our group rules is that anyone may ask someone else anything. If someone doesn't want to answer a question, he is not required to do so. He is, however, expected to say directly what he is unwilling to answer.

Before clients start group, we give them information about the structure, expectations and ground rules of the group. We tell them that they will probably see many unusual things, and that they are to ask for information when they don't understand what is happening. Even with the instructions, they are likely to play it cool, and not ask. We usually assume that a new client has questions she is not asking, and confront gently and appropriately. Recognizing the client's body language, stating the unasked question and having the client repeat the question aloud are all helpful.

Uninhibited preschool children ask many questions in their attempt to understand the world. Clear, honest and age-appropriate answers are what they need in response. Children in dysfunctional families do not like to bother grown-ups; instead of asking, they try to figure things out for themselves. As adults, they may be highly intuitive. Unfortunately, they seldom check to find out whether their perceptions are correct. This may lead to problems, when they act on information that does not have much to do with reality.

Jan, a 48-year-old grandmother, won't ask her doctor about specific pains she is having; she believes her doctor knows what is wrong with her and what to do about it. It takes a long conversation with her, about how doctors get information, before she is willing to let me help her write out what the doctor will need to know. She is still much too scared to simply tell him; she believes that he would put her down the way her father did, if she tries to tell him about her own experience.

Initially, clients practice asking in the protected setting of the therapist's office or the group, where there are specific agreements about what will (and won't) happen in response. Often, we will suggest that the client ask, "What would you do if I . . . (eg., asked you why you're frowning)?" We also suggest they ask questions about the conclusions and beliefs they are holding: "Do you like me?" "Are you mad at me?" "Is he going to hurt someone because he's mad?" or "Do I have to go away if I don't do what you want?" It is vital that the client get clear, direct, understandable answers to the questions; sarcastic responses are forbidden and confronted immediately if they are given.

Later, we instruct clients to practice outside the therapy setting, to break the habit of mind-reading to determine what others want.

We give the following instructions: "When you suspect that people want something, ask them what they want instead of guessing and automatically getting it for them. Ask your husband whether he wants you to get a cup of coffee for him, instead of automatically bringing it to him. Ask whether your wife wants you to pick her up, when she hints that she would like a ride. When your children give you long tales containing implications that you should help them in some way, ask why they are telling you about the situation, or ask if they want you to do something about it. After others have made their requests, decide whether you are willing to do as they ask."

Adult Children expect people to treat them the way their parents did. They have trouble believing that any environment is safe. They can maintain this belief because they neither seek out nor take in information about their current reality. We confront the belief system by encouraging them to experiment with healthy information-gathering behavior.

When we propose some changes in group policy, *Tammy* withdraws and sulks, muttering about leaving treatment. We ask her if she is having feelings about the proposed changes, and learn that she has several ideas about it that she is afraid to say. She doesn't believe us when we tell her that it is okay for her to say what she thinks and how she feels. She is certain that we will get mad at her if she disagrees with us, and she is convinced that it wouldn't do any good anyway. We eventually convince her to speak up; when we incorporate one of her ideas in the policy, she begins to learn that not everyone will treat her the way her parents did.

We invite clients to experiment, during treatment sessions, with behaviors they considered bad and dangerous as children, in order to get different, healthy feedback — corrective parenting. They may interrupt; comment on what they notice, even if it's impolite; break rules; and call attention to themselves. These experiments are done *only* in the treatment situation, where everyone understands the specific agreements that are made about what the client will do.

Regressive Treatment: Parenting The Inner Child

In direct corrective parenting, we define the above agreement as "a contract to be four years old, and to behave the way a normal child of that age would." Responses to the client's behavior must contain the kind of feedback that would be appropriate for healthy parenting of a four-year-old child. Some examples include:

1. Clear and caring explanations of reasons for rules —
   "We don't throw hard things, because they could hurt someone, including you."
   "People are not for hitting. It wouldn't be okay for someone else to hit you, and it's not okay for you to do it to someone else."
   "You put away the things you played with so that they can be found when you or someone else wants them; no one wants to clean up after you; you wouldn't want to have to pick up the things that someone else left out."
2. Statements of cause-and-effect connections —
   "You didn't make her (another client in the group) mad; she's mad because of something she's remembering that happened to her."
   "I'm not going away because you were mad at me; I'm going on vacation because I want some time to rest and play, and I will come back in two weeks, when I'm through."
3. Reasonable, clear and consistent consequences —
   "If you don't pick up the toys, you will have to stand in the corner for as long as it takes someone else to pick them up."
   "If you throw that again, we will take it away until you decide not to throw it anymore."
4. Truthful and appropriate answers to difficult questions —
   Q: "Will you be my Daddy?"
   A: "I'll be the Daddy to your Inner Child, when you are being little in group, so that you can learn to take care of that part of you when you are grown-up."

When a client is being four, he often asks questions about his own feelings or about the emotions that he sees displayed by others in the group. We respond with the information about feelings described in Chapter 8, modified into language that is appropriate for a child.

A useful exercise for people focusing on issues from this stage uses Levin's "Affirmations for Power and Identity". These affirmations can either be assigned as a "homework" writing exercise, or the client can ask for someone to say these things to them in the group:

1. "You can be powerful and still have needs."
2. "You don't have to act scared or sick or sad or mad to get taken care of."
3. "It's okay for you to explore who you are."
4. "It's important for you to find out what you're about."
5. "It's okay to imagine things without being afraid you'll make them come true."
6. "It's okay to find out the consequences of your own behavior."

When a client presents issues in treatment concerning sexuality or sex role identity, we look to see if she is operating on the basis of the information of a four-year-old. When this is the case, we see to it that her Inner Child gets the necessary information. We suggest that she "be four", and encourage her to ask all the questions she wants from that position. We will often read to her, using a picture storybook we have found to be especially helpful: *Where Did I Come From?* by Peter Mayle.

Giving Up Magic

The Adult Child, like the preschool child, usually believes in magic; specifically, that his thoughts and feelings can make things happen in the world around him. The client who shows that he is operating with these beliefs is challenged to actually test it out in group. He is instructed to sit there and feel and think specific things as hard as he can, and see what actually happens. He is also encouraged to ask people why they do things, particularly things that they do in response to him.

It is often an important discovery for the Adult Child to get in touch with the anger that he has been suppressing since childhood. Having the client confront the parent, in fantasy, is an especially useful technique for this part of the therapeutic work. Experiencing the acceptance of others when these previously hidden feelings come to the surface is often a dramatic boost to the client's self-esteem.

Cathartic release of anger, as a treatment technique, must be used carefully with clients who still believe in magic. It is very easy for the client to come to believe that if only they get angry enough, the parent will change. The therapist must lead the client into recognizing the hopelessness of ever having the power to change the parent (or to control the situation by being good). When the client understands the magic wish, and gives it up, a healthy grief reaction signifies the conclusion of this work.

Susan did some intense anger work about her father's repeated abuse and her mother's lack of protection. She demanded that her mother take care of her, and had the satisfaction of expressing the feelings she had to suppress as a child. This experience was cathartic and useful. Now her mother is seriously ill, and Susan is terrified that Mother will die before giving Susan the nurturing she never got. After careful direct questioning, Susan finally recognizes that, even if her mother lives, she can still *never* get the nurturing she missed from her mother. She hides under a blanket, trying to avoid the feelings. Finally, she starts to cry convulsively, and is held and comforted while she weeps for the next hour.

15

WORKING WITH FEELINGS — PART 3

The Adult Child cannot be considered to have recovered from his Co-dependence until he has grieved: he must grieve, not only for the loss of a normal childhood, but also for all the normal adult experiences he missed out on as a result of his childhood losses.

In order to complete the grief process, the Adult Child must first recognize that there *was* a loss. He must acknowledge that the loss is irretrievable, and stop trying to prevent, control, undo or deny it. He must be able to feel emotions in general, and sadness in particular. He must be willing to express the sad feelings overtly, to another person, and accept the other's support and comforting. He must then learn to live in a new environment, one that lacks the lost object or experience. Finally, he must withdraw his emotional energy from the loss, so that he can use that energy to invest in new experiences.

Resistance To Grief Work

The process of doing the necessary grief work is frequently blocked by the specific effect of unmet developmental needs.

Bonding Stage

Grief can be blocked by unmet needs from the Bonding Stage. The only defense an infant has for handling the pain of not getting his needs met is to shut down the experience of the needs. If the Adult Child did this when he was an infant, the resulting passivity makes it very difficult for him to identify and experience later feelings of loss. He may be able to understand the loss intellectually, but feels blocked from actually experiencing the emotion.

The Adult Child with significant problems arising from the Bonding Stage needs to release the rage at not getting taken care of, before he is in a position to do the grief work. The process of releasing that rage is described in detail in Chapter 12.

Many clients experience deep, sobbing sadness when they complete a session of rage work. We physically hold them and support them in their grief. We typically affirm, "What you are angry about really happened. I'm sorry it happened, and it's really okay to feel all the sadness that's there." This support often leads to more tears, as the client recognizes that he has been treating his own Inner Child as he was treated himself. The grief process is completed when the client allows himself to accept nurturing from others, and incorporates it so that he can nurture his own Inner Child.

While *Stan* was in the process of doing his grief work, he woke up in the middle of the night, feeling scared and little. He took hold of a stuffed animal that represented to him his infant Inner Child, and told himself, "You're safe here; I'm big and I'll take care of you. Nothing bad can happen to you when I'm here, and I'll never leave you alone." After a few minutes, he fell asleep again and woke at his usual time, feeling safe and refreshed.

Exploratory Stage

Grief can be blocked by unmet needs from the Exploratory Stage. The experience of engulfment or abandonment interferes with the development of a sense of a whole self. As a result, the Adult Child with problems from this stage experiences painful feelings as overwhelming and intolerable. He can't recognize that such feelings are only a *part* of his reality; from the position of his fragmented sense of self, he experiences that the pain is all there is, with no memory or expectation of relief.

Separation Stage

Grief can be blocked by unmet needs from the Separation Stage. Both complying and rebelling keep the Adult Child out of touch with his deepest feelings. Someone without a sense of his own identity and individuality is too busy adapting to the needs and feelings of others to notice much about his own. The Adult Child who is overtly or covertly rebellious may take the information that he needs to grieve as a parental attempt to direct and control him, and will resist doing the work.

Abandonment Depression

Many people who have not completed the individuation processes of the Exploratory and Separation Stages may go through a process that looks like grief, but has some important differences. Grief is a process of dealing with the loss of something or someone that is outside of oneself. When a person has not individuated, there is both a fragmentation of the sense of self and a confusion between what is "out there" and what is "in here". As a result, a loss may be experienced as a loss of part or all of one's *self*.

Abbie has been immersing herself in therapy, support groups, reading and intensive workshops, trying to heal her extensive Adult Child issues. After much denial, she remembers early scenes of repeated sexual abuse by her father and brothers. The recognition of the reality of what she lived through is devastating to her; she sees that she has been hiding the truth from herself for years.

The realization that *nothing* in her childhood was loving or caring is almost overwhelming to her. She feels like she has no idea of who or what she really is, and all she can think of for several weeks is how rotten she feels.

It is difficult for someone with a good sense of his own wholeness to appreciate the extraordinary pain experienced by someone with this problem. It is like facing an amputation without anesthetic. Because of the degree of pain involved, many clients are resistant to doing the kind of Inner Child work that

will, inevitably, expose this issue. When it does surface, the client
will experience what is called the "abandonment depression" in
James Masterson's *Psychotherapy of the Borderline Adult.*

As difficult as it is for the client, the appearance of these intensely
painful feelings is a positive sign that the therapeutic process is
moving forward. Clients need information and support from the
therapist, so that they can allow themselves to feel these feelings,
instead of trying frantically to find a way to feel better immediately.
These feelings must be experienced to be completed.

It is tempting for the therapist to suggest activities that will
distract the client from the pain and help him feel better. This isn't
helpful in the long run, because it reinforces substitute behaviors,
ie., the defenses against the pain, rather than supporting the client
in working through it.

When a client is dealing with the abandonment depression, we
encourage daily brief (two- or three-minute) phone calls, in which
we remind him that there is more to him than his pain. We
reassure him that the process he is going through is healthy and
normal, and encourage him to stick with it so that he can come out
the other side.

We will remind him that he has the ability to use his Adult to
keep the necessary commitments in his life, but we suggest that he
temporarily cut back on unnecessary activities in order to take
time for his own internal process. In group, we provide physical
nurturing, and we support the client in staying with the feelings
until the process is complete. This may take weeks or months; the
feelings of overwhelming grief gradually diminish to occasional
sadness, and eventually stop recurring.

Socialization Stage

Grief can be blocked by unmet needs from the Socialization
Stage. Magical thinking can keep the Adult Child stuck with the
idea that "if only I do this (whatever 'this' is) long enough, I can
help or change my parents, make my world safe or get my needs
met." Magical thinking can usually be recognized when the client
appears unwilling to give up an idea or behavior that clearly
doesn't work. This pattern can take a variety of forms.

Susan's Inner Child had been holding on to the magical idea
that, as long as her mother was still alive, there was a chance that
her mother would eventually nurture her. When she used her
Adult to look at the situation, Susan knew that her mother was an

untreated Co-dependent, who always demanded that Susan discount her own needs entirely in favor of meeting mother's needs. She also knew that her mother's behavior had been growing steadily more demanding, and that her mother was dying.

Susan's magical belief system retained significant power over her Adult information because of the dysfunctional parenting she received in the Socialization Stage. She was repeatedly told that she was responsible for what other people did and felt; her sense of omnipotence was reinforced in an intensely pathological way. When she was sexually molested by a neighbor at the age of three, for example, her father beat her because "she made the neighbor do it." Mother allowed the beating.

The corrective parenting she was receiving helped her to accept that she was not specifically responsible for the molestation; but the general belief system, that she *was* responsible for the bad things that happened to her, was still deep and pervasive. Her response to her mother's imminent death showed us that we still needed to help her realize she had no magical abilities. Susan's Inner Child frantically drove her to try to keep her mother alive. She desperately tried to avoid accepting the reality of the situation. Susan finally allowed herself to begin the grieving process when she accepted our strong confrontation that she never had received and never would receive her mother's love.

Magical thinking can sometimes be exposed, releasing the grief, by having the client exaggerate the distorted thought process underlying the repetitive pattern.

Jackie, age 37, wants our approval for her continuing, repetitive anger at her mother. She brings "nasty and threatening" letters from her mother to group to justify her position and show us how awful her mother really is. The letters seem fairly ordinary: expressions of disappointment that Jackie hasn't called or written in months, or news of successful or joyful events among family and friends.

We experiment with having Jackie tell her mother (in fantasy), "I'll never forgive you for how you treated me when I was little!" Jackie starts to elaborate: "You bitch, you're still trying to control me and live your life through me by making me do things your way! If I forgive you, I'll have to do what you want."

When we hear this, we ask Jackie to explain to her mother, still in the fantasy, more about how she must stay angry at her in order to keep from following her instructions. Jackie goes on in this vein for a while, then stops, turns to us and says, "I don't have to do those things. I'm in charge of me now. I really did have to do them when I was little, to keep her from locking me out of the house. I was powerless then, and I couldn't change her." She starts to sob, allowing herself to feel the healing grief instead of the anger.

Supporting Grief Work

Once the blocks have been released and the client starts to grieve, the therapist's job is primarily supportive. Many fine books have been written on the grief process itself, and we will not elaborate on that information here. A superb book for Adult Children, for example, is *After the Tears* by Lori Dwinnel and Jane Middelton-Moz.

Sometimes a grief process can be hindered or blocked by Parent beliefs and rules about feelings. The client may start to feel appropriate grief about a loss and then try to stop the feeling, because he believes it is weak to feel, or that the feelings are lasting "too long". New information and support is usually sufficient to overcome this kind of obstacle to feeling.

Don's wife left him, taking their four-year-old son with her. He tried to drown his feelings with alcohol, because he believed that crying about his loss was a sign of weakness. When we told him it was normal and okay to grieve, he was surprised, and accepted the permission.

When *Connie* separated from her husband, she blocked off her sadness with frantic activity. When we confronted the resulting agitation, she declared that she shouldn't feel sad, because the change was good for her — and after all, she had asked him to leave. When we told her that it was okay to grieve the loss of something that had been important, even though it was something that had been bad for her, she accepted our invitation and let herself feel the very real grief.

Two weeks after *Jimmie's* father died, he was criticizing himself because he was having trouble concentrating on his work. We explained the grieving process to him, and he allowed himself to experience it.

There are many ways to help clients acknowledge their losses and experience the pain of those losses. Once a client is experiencing this pain, he needs permission to keep feeling it as long as it persists. This permission can be expressed verbally: "It's okay to feel; you can feel and express your feelings here. You don't have to shut off your feelings to take care of someone else. You don't have to go away. It's important to be with someone who cares about you when you feel this way."

The permission to grieve can also be expressed physically, simply by sitting with the person or by gently touching or holding him while he feels the pain.

If we feel sad about the client's loss, we may share our own feelings. Sometimes this sharing is startling and healing to the client. Sometimes crying with a client about a profound loss feels like the only possible thing to do.

After the client has felt the pain, he may ask, "Now what?" Although it isn't possible to recapture a lost childhood, the unmet needs may still persist. The next step is to encourage the client to plan appropriate ways to experience getting those needs met. The corrective parenting experiences described throughout this book are a method for allowing the Adult Child to have such experiences. It's never too late for anyone to have a happy childhood.

CHAPTER 16

LATENCY STAGE

Sam panics at work when he is given a complicated task, and phones the therapist for help. His Inner Child is hearing his alcoholic father yelling at him for being stupid, and he feels immobilized with fear. The therapist reminds him that nobody around him is treating him the way his father did, and asks him if there is any part of the task he does understand. She suggests he start with what he does know, and tells him that it's okay to ask for help with the parts he doesn't understand, if he needs it. Later, in group, he reports that he had no problem accomplishing the task.

Sam is trying to do his work by following a dysfunctional set of rules about how to do tasks. His rules are: (1) that he should already know how to do any task assigned to him, (2) that he should do it perfectly the first time and (3) that he deserves abuse if he has any difficulty. Sam is typical of the Adult Children who "guess at what normal is", "have difficulty in following a project through from beginning to end", and "judge themselves without mercy", described by Janet Woititz in *Adult Children of Alcoholics.*

Healthy Development

The developmental task of the Latency Stage, from approximately age six years to puberty, is to develop a set of workable rules to live by (a Parent Ego State, in Transactional Analysis terms). In order for Parent rules to be useful and workable, the child needs to be able to *think* about them; he needs to learn to connect the rules with the reasons for them. **He must learn that the reasons for rules are more important than the rules themselves, and that following rules is a method for making things work.**

In a healthy setting, children normally learn to think about rules by arguing about them. Ideally, arguing challenges the parents to clarify and communicate the reasons for the rules, rather than allowing them simply to force the child to comply with them without thinking. In addition to challenging the parents' thinking, arguing keeps the child from having to simply swallow the parents' rules without any consideration of his own point of view.

A healthy school-age child will challenge most rules he encounters. He spends many hours arguing with parents and peers about the "right" way to do things. Rules such as "nine o'clock is bedtime", "You have to keep your room clean", "Your homework has to be done before you can watch TV", etc., are met with responses such as, "I'm not sleepy," "My friend doesn't have to," and "The special kids' program will be over by then."

The parent can help the child to understand the reasons for the rules by explaining why the child should do as the parent suggests or commands. The child needs encouragement to state his own reasons for his objections and, ultimately, to work out a solution that takes both sets of reasons into account.

Because the grade school years are a time of rapid learning and skill development, there needs to be much discussion about the "right" way to do things. Parents of Latency Stage children need to be willing to argue, explain and negotiate over hundreds of issues. This can be a frustrating, time-consuming task, but if it is not done, the child will have trouble learning to think about the reasons for rules.

David, age seven, didn't want to wear a belt with his school pants. His parents said he had to, and he pointed out that his pants wouldn't fall down without the belt. They said that pants with belt loops were supposed to be worn with a belt; he said the belt was too hot. They said the pants didn't look good with empty belt loops; he said they looked fine to him, that he liked them that way. They said the teachers at school might think they weren't good parents if he wasn't dressed properly, ie., with a belt.

He finally agreed to wear the belt, but took it off the instant he returned home from school. He accepted the rule of "You should dress appropriately for the occasion", and continues (15 years later) to choose clothes that are socially appropriate. The next argument was about where to put the belt when you take it off.

The school-age child is strongly motivated to learn the mechanics of the world. She needs to learn how to get things to work, and why they work that way. She needs information, explanations and opportunities to learn from her own efforts. Children learn how to do things most effectively when they think about how to produce the result they want, rather than when they have to think about how to follow exact orders. Appropriate parenting gives a child room to find out what works *for her,* with assistance in problem-solving when needed.

Jill, age 10, wanted to sew a dress for herself. Mother offered to help, but Jill adamantly refused. She drew an outline of a dress that fit her on a piece of fabric, cut it out and sewed it up. It turned out to be much too small.

A few weeks later, Jill was ready to try again. This time, because it had not worked the way she wanted it to before, she was willing to accept help in figuring out how to cut it to the proper size. She then sewed it herself, and wore it proudly. Mother didn't comment on the uneven stitching and hemline. Jill liked making skirts and got better at it; she learned to use a pattern in a Home Economics class when she was thirteen. Years later, she still is untroubled by mistakes she makes when she learns to do something new.

Dysfunctional Development

Children raised in dysfunctional families may have to alternate between trying to follow rigid and impossible rules and having no consistent rules at all. They are often forced to follow orders, so that they learn to use rules, rather than reasons, to guide their behavior. This makes it difficult for them to solve problems when the rules don't work, or when they don't have a specific rule for the situation.

Jeffrey's fearful, isolated family taught him never to talk to strangers. When, at seven, he became separated from his mother

in a department store, the rule he had been forced to incorporate
prevented him from asking any clerks for assistance. After a long,
frightening afternoon, his mother found him and spanked him for
getting lost; she never did teach him *what to do* if he were lost.

A child growing up in a dysfunctional family is often so afraid of
any type of conflict that she will never even consider challenging
a parental rule. She will do her very best to obey all rules, whether
stated or implied, in the hope that doing so will maintain some
peace in the chaotic family.

Because many of the parental rules conflict with each other, and
because the child is not really in control of the adults' behavior,
her efforts to keep the peace are doomed to failure. She sees the
failure as a sign of her own inadequacy, and tries even harder to
do better.

Jeanne worked hard in school, got all A's and hurried home
after school to help her mother with the younger children. She
was quiet and supportive whenever her mother threatened
suicide, and helped her mother keep an affair secret from her
father. She felt devastated and guilty when mother deserted the
family when Jeanne was 12.

As penitence for her failure to keep her mother happy, and to try
to please her father, she took on the responsibility of caring for
seven younger children. As an adult businesswoman, she still feels
guilty if anything goes wrong, even if it has nothing to do with her.
She works unrealistically long hours, many more than anyone else,
because she is "responsible".

Children of dysfunctional families have no opportunity to learn
to think about the reasons for rules or to learn to negotiate with
others about alternative ways of doing things. When a child does
take the risk of challenging a parental rule, he may be defined as
bad or uncontrollable. Instead or arguing with him, or explaining
the reasons for anything, the parent may let him do exactly as he
pleases. The parent may then alternate between lack of response
and angry, even violent, attempts to force obedience. In *For Your
Own Good,* Alice Miller gives chilling examples of how people
raised in dysfunctional homes perpetuate the harmful and
repressive rules they were forced to incorporate as children.

Sam grew up in a large family. His Co-dependent mother was ill
when he entered school, and when he wanted to do things his
own way, she didn't even try to stop him. She complained to Sam's
father about how uncontrollable he was. Father didn't pay much

attention when he was sober, but when he was drunk he verbally and physically abused Sam for being so "bad".

School-age children learn rules about how to do things and which things are appropriate for them to do, by observation and practice. Because children in dysfunctional families often overtly reject their parental models, they search elsewhere for the "right" way to do things. They look to the media, to entertainment and sports figures for their role models. Because they can't interact directly with these people, they tend to idealize them and incorporate even more unrealistic expectations of themselves. When they cannot meet these inappropriate standards, they see it as a result of their own personal inadequacy.

Flo rejected both her passive and timid mother and her domineering, overbearing and abusive father as role models. After a short and disastrous first marriage, she read women's magazines, which explained how to be a "Superwoman". She managed to get a graduate degree, a new husband (who left all responsibility for the household to her), two additional children and a business to run. She reported feeling tired, guilty, inadequate and severely depressed when she started treatment.

Many Adult Children were expected to know how to do complicated tasks with no instruction or help whatsoever.

Bill, at six, had to figure out how to take two buses to the dentist's office alone.

When *Roxy,* at eight, had to take on the grocery shopping for a family of six, her mother told her "You can do it," with no further instructions.

Robert, seven, became the man of the family when his parents divorced. He took over keeping the furnace running, the snow shoveled, the lawn cut, the leaves raked and the family pets cared for.

As grown-ups, these Adult Children typically take on jobs they are not trained to do, feel terrified and gradually figure out how to do the task by themselves. It never occurs to them to ask for help or instruction. They are certain that they are dumb or inadequate if they can't do something that someone else can do; **they don't recognize that others went through a learning or training process.**

Many avoid trying new things, because they fear others will learn about their inadequacy if they don't perform perfectly the first time. They have never had the opportunity to learn how to learn.

Len started a graduate school program and spent days studying for a test. He "only" got a B; for the next exam he spent twice as long studying. He still only earned a B and was ready to drop out of graduate school.

When we discussed it, we found that he studied by trying to memorize everything indiscriminately. He had never learned to organize or prioritize information. Instruction in simple study skills helped him get the A's he felt he needed.

Larry was never able to complete his work projects on time. Even though he worked long hours, trying very hard to please his supervisor, he almost lost his job. When the supervisor finally asked how Larry was going about the work, he discovered that Larry was unfamiliar with many of the resources that would make the work easier. Larry had never asked for help; he assumed he had to create everything himself, and didn't want to "look stupid".

Most Adult Children have some developmental deficits from the Latency Stage. Because problems in each stage will affect each subsequent stage, difficulties at any or all of the preceeding stages will have an impact here. The Adult Child who didn't explore as a baby, rebel as a two-year-old or ask questions as a preschooler is not likely to argue during the grade-school years.

Treatment Implications

The Adult Child needs to learn to argue using reasons and then to negotiate; in this way, he can learn to incorporate a healthy, reasonable Parent Ego State. Before this learning can take place, however, it is often necessary to deal with the problems that came from earlier developmental stages. If we attempt to help the Adult Child learn to handle conflict and disagreement, without addressing earlier developmental issues, we are often ineffective.

Sarah, a paralegal assistant, believes that she is expected to work right through her lunch hour. She is angry and feels like resigning, but she is afraid the problem will recur in another job. When we find out that she has not discussed the problem with her employer, she quickly agrees to do so. When she reports later that she didn't carry out her plan, we discover that she is terrified of asking for what she wants or even of letting her boss know that she has a problem.

As we investigate further, she tells us about having been sexually abused by her alcoholic father as a toddler, and deciding to never call attention to herself. The early problems make it almost impossible, at this point, for her to learn to negotiate. She has much work to do at earlier developmental stages before she can take on this task.

When clients have learned to ask for what they want, explore, say *no* and ask questions, they are probably ready to learn to negotiate. The group setting provides ample opportunities to learn about negotiation; working out disagreements in the group is both modeled and encouraged.

We model the process by openly expressing and resolving our own disagreements (as co-therapists) within the group setting. We encourage working out disagreements when we notice nonverbal signals that a client may be disagreeing about something. If that happens, we invite and encourage the direct expression of the problem, whether it is with us or with another client.

We use these events as opportunities to give information about the reasons for conflict, eg., "People have different needs and different ideas about how to do things", and about methods for dealing with conflict, eg., "Find out what each person wants and figure out what it makes sense to do".

Often clients will look upset in response to disagreement or conflict in the group, especially if the disagreement is between us. Most Adult Children have never seen a conflict resolved in a healthy way, in which the needs of each person are taken into account and solutions are sought where everybody can win. They believe that all conflict is necessarily destructive, and they fear the consequences when disagreements come to the surface. Clients have often told us that they wait for one of us to hit or scream at the other when we disagree. When clients have the opportunity to witness healthy conflict resolution, they can more easily learn how to do it themselves.

When the disagreement is between one of us and a client, it is often necessary to coach the client through the discussion. In a co-therapy situation, one of the therapists can act as coach; in an ongoing group, a more experienced client can take this role (and is usually delighted to do so).

The focus of the coaching is often to keep reminding the client to give the reasons for his position. The therapist must also give reasons and must be willing to consider shifting his position. The coach may also continue to invite the client to propose alternatives, so that all parties involved in the argument can be satisfied.

We have argued with clients about a wide variety of topics:

- "I think the group should meet later."
- "I don't think we should meet when it's snowing."
- "I should get to work next; I've been waiting longer than she has."
- "Why shouldn't I take advantage of that [slightly dishonest] deal?"
- "I don't think I should have to do something for the group, just because I was late again."
- "I don't think I need to argue."
- "I don't need therapy any more."

While we argue, we usually acknowledge them for taking the risk of standing up for their beliefs. We always search for a win-win solution.

Curt, who had almost completed his treatment, proposed missing group for an extended period of time, so that he could study for his martial arts exam; he had a special preparation class that met at the same time as his therapy group. We did not accept his original plan, and, after much discussion of alternatives, we agreed on a compromise plan that worked for everyone. Curt agreed to give up his space in group, but would come at least once a month, when someone else was absent, to do his remaining therapy work. Having this discussion, in which his point of view and ours were both treated as valid, was what he needed to do to integrate the work he had been doing in therapy. He carried out his agreement and completed his goals in Tae Kwan Do and in therapy.

Problems stemming from the Latency Stage of development often look similar to those that stem from the Separation Stage. The similarity is that both may be resistant and argumentative; the major difference is that the Separation Stage Inner Child can only give "I don't want to" as a reason. Occasionally a client will start to argue and get stuck in the oppositional position. When this happens, we ask the client to check with his Inner Child and see if he needs to have his reasons listened to, or just needs to be accepted even though he doesn't want what we want.

Some clients will neither argue with nor follow rules or directions; these are the Adult Children who learned to pay lip service to what was expected of them, and then to do whatever they wanted, knowing that no one would care enough to notice.

It is important to confront this pattern; learning to argue and negotiate is essential for clearing up problems in any relationship.

Flo would state what she wanted, and would assume that Roy's silence meant that he agreed: she would think he was coming home from dinner, for example, because she told him what time to be there. If the time didn't fit his schedule, he would just not show up; he had no awareness that she thought there was an agreement, because he knew he hadn't made one. She would be furious, and they would fight. They are now learning to state their disagreements immediately, and then reach clear agreements that they commit to. Their fights are diminishing.

In addition to learning to argue, Adult Children need the opportunity to learn how to do things in a way that works for them, instead of in the "right" way. Levin offers the following affirmations to counter the messages learned in a dysfunctional family.

- "It's okay for you to learn how to do things your own way, and to have your own morals and methods."
- "You can think before you make that your way."
- "Trust your feelings to guide you."
- "You can do it your way."
- "You don't have to suffer to get what you need."
- "It's okay to disagree."

Many Adult Children have very little information about how and why other people do things. Once they recognize that they need that kind of information, it is important that they get it. Once they have both their own experience and the information from others' experience, they can make choices about what is right for them.

As a child, *Jack* would sneak into his room and hope no one would know he was home. He didn't learn that most people said, "Hello" to others when they came in until his roommates got angry with him for being secretive.

Cory needed to know that her supervisor's feedback contained information that she could use to improve her performance — instead of a message that she was incompetent and bad.

Larry needed to know that he didn't have to leave because he was angry at someone, that healthy people discussed their anger.

Judy needed to know that calling people racist epithets was not the only way to show her displeasure. She had to learn to say what she wanted changed.

Often Adult Children are unaware that they lack information; they just heap abuse on themselves when their efforts do not produce the unrealistic results they expect. The therapist needs to be alert for this possibility and offer alternatives if the client berates herself.

Much of *Bonnie's* self-criticism occurred when she was working or doing household tasks; there was a constant internal chatter in her mind, saying things like, "Don't do it like that, Stupid . . . You'll never learn . . . What a klutz, you're so clumsy . . . Can't you do anything right, etc., etc."

Bonnie was able to identify that the voice in her head sounded just like her father, and, indeed, he had talked to her in just that way when she was in grade school. We had a long discussion with her about how learning how to do things always involves making mistakes. We helped her to notice that she wasn't paying attention to what she was learning when she was paying attention to the voice in her head, and that, in fact, she could choose to ignore the voice.

In the group setting, we gave her a set of small beanbags and an instruction book on how to juggle, with the assignment to practice making mistakes in the middle of the room. As Bonnie became engrossed in this apparently frivolous exercise, she began to recognize for herself that she was gradually learning how to do the task; more importantly, she saw that the mistakes she made gave her the information about what she needed to practice.

Bonnie's increasing delight with her own abilities eventually drowned out the critical voice in her head. As we expected, from our map of the developmental tasks of the Latency Stage, she rapidly generalized the idea of being able to learn from her mistakes.

Regressive Treatment: Parenting The Inner Child

Direct corrective parenting can also be a useful approach to problems from the Latency Stage. When the client agrees to activate his school-age Inner Child, he then talks to the therapist about concerns and needs and experiences appropriate to that age. The therapist provides encouragement for him to discover options and make his own decisions. When the Inner Child is found to be lacking some important information, the therapist may provide it.

Sometimes it can be useful for a client, in his Latency age Inner Child, to work on a project with the therapist (eg., build a model airplane), discussing together the various ways to approach the task. Discussions about the probable consequences of different courses of action also help the client learn about the reasons for making different choices.

After his telephone conversation with Laurie, *Sam* brought a model airplane to group, so that he could get some parenting about how to handle problems with doing tasks. He decided to be eight, got started on the task and soon appeared to be confused and upset.

The therapist discovered that Sam's model was designed for children age ten and older. She showed him the information, and said that the job might be too advanced for him now. She asked him what he wanted to do, and gave him several choices: (1) he could try to do the best he could with the model as it was, (2) he could keep playing with the pieces of the model without trying to put it together or (3) he could find some other project that he could do. He happily chose another task.

Treatment of problems from this stage is complete when the client learns how to handle differences and disagreements by negotiation and consensus. Negotiation is a complex skill that involves identifying needs, discovering options and reaching satisfaction. Considerable practice is required to take oneself *and* others into account when solving problems. In therapy, we can help a client practice and understand some of the basic principles, and apply them in his own situation.

The first step in learning to negotiate is to define the problems and goals clearly. We encourage the client to determine what each person wants before proposing a solution to the problem. Many conflicts are created when people fight about the "right" solution to a problem that has not been defined in terms of needs. (See *Getting to Yes* by Fisher and Urey, for an excellent discussion of this point of view.)

We then ask the client to come up with options that will take into account the desires of all parties to the negotiation. Once he has some options, we ask him to discuss them with the other people involved, to see if he can reach a win-win agreement.

When appropriate, we suggest that the details be put in writing, stating who will do what by when, where, and what will happen if the agreement isn't kept. This forces clients to clarify and renegotiate points they might have missed earlier.

Finally, we remind them that the purpose of agreements is to serve the people involved, so that they can be renegotiated by mutual consent at any time.

Learning to negotiate agreements that take everyone's needs into account has a very positive impact on self-esteem and the sense of competency. The Inner Child who has successfully completed the developmental tasks of the Latency Stage usually feels confident and excited about being in the world.

CHAPTER 17

ADOLESCENCE

When *Cory* was 14, her father died and her alcoholic mother was placed in a mental institution. Cory reacted with drinking, drug abuse, promiscuity and compulsive overeating. Now, at 30, she is seven years into recovery.

In therapy, she has learned to express her feelings instead of overeating, and layers of protective fat have disappeared. She tries dating for the first time in years, and is confused about how to act with a man. Co-dependent men are attracted to her, because she is a good listener. After a while, she realizes that when she talks about herself, the men are seldom interested. In therapy, she begins to ask questions about what men think about and expect from women.

Cory didn't have the opportunity to deal with the ordinary problems of adolescence when she was a teenager. Now that she has almost completed the work of healing her Inner Child, she needs support and encouragement to incorporate a healthy sexuality into her life. She also needs to separate from her therapeutic "family" in a way that allows her to feel that she is not abandoned, that there is a "home" she can return to if she needs it.

Healthy Development

At puberty, it is as if a complete person, with well-functioning Parent, Adult and Child Ego States, is reborn into a new body, thus creating a whole new relationship with the world. Even though she has already traversed the earlier developmental stages, and learned ways to deal with each of the issues, she must now relearn them as a sexually mature individual who needs to relate to a world larger than family and schoolmates.

Not only does the adolescent have to "recycle" all of the developmental stages, she needs to do so while also learning to function independently of the family. She no longer needs "parenting" to provide psychologically, what she does not yet have herself. She *does* need guidance and support to accomplish her main developmental task: learning how to use and integrate and restructure what she should already have.

This task is accomplished gradually, as the adolescent recycles all of the earlier developmental stages:

1. The adolescent who has been responsible for making her own lunch for years may suddenly demand that her mother feed her.
2. He may switch in minutes from claiming that he just wants to be left alone to demanding extra nurturing; he then berates his parents for not keeping up with the switch.
3. The peer group, rather than the family, becomes the place to belong, and young people try to demonstrate that belonging by following rigid dress codes, looking as much like each other and as different from grown-ups as possible.
4. A previously courteous and considerate youngster may suddenly become inconsiderate and rebellious, and alternate between these behaviors from one moment to the next.
5. Family values are argumentatively challenged, as the adolescent impulsively explores new experiences that may be unfamiliar, dangerous and frightening to the parents.

The parent is continuously faced with having to choose between the possible mistakes of treating a mature youngster like a child or giving a childish one more responsibility than he can handle appropriately. Even in the healthiest of families, parenting an adolescent feels like balancing on a tightrope. Communicating Levin's healthy messages to a rapidly changing adolescent is a real challenge. It is difficult to consistently remind an adolescent that:

1. "You can be a sexual person and still have needs."
2. "It's okay to be responsible for your own needs, feelings and behavior."
3. "It's okay to be on your own."
4. "You're welcome to come home again."
5. "My love goes with you."

As the earlier developmental stages are recycled, there is a new opportunity for the adolescent to learn to meet those developmental needs in a healthy way. Because the issues of each stage are energized again, new learning is possible.

Problems and distortions created at earlier stages will recur, possibly with more energy, and certainly with the potential for even more destructive expression. An adolescent has more options for dangerous behavior, and fewer parental controls, than the young child has.

Dysfunctional Development

A distorted attempt to handle unmet developmental needs can lead to more serious consequences for the adolescent. The untreated dysfunctional family can rarely support an adolescent in meeting these recycled needs.

The compliant family heroine may attempt once more to become independent, by daring to disagree with her parents or by attempting to be like her peers. If these attempts are met with heavy-handed control by the parents, the heroine may retreat into a sullen acceptance of her fate, possibly escaping into an early marriage.

The adolescent used to the Scapegoat role may recycle his attempts at autonomy by becoming even more unmanageable, and may abuse chemicals or try other life-threatening behaviors. When the parents react with their own unresolved rage, further uproars follow. The pattern continues until the adolescent leaves home — usually by angrily "slamming the door behind him", vowing never to return.

Some adolescents become so enmeshed in the family that they see no possibility of escape. Eating disorders are often a signal that this underground struggle is occurring. In any event, the adolescent rarely gets what she needs to smoothly complete the process of emancipation from the family.

Treatment Implications

When treating the Adult Child's adolescent issues, we attempt to distinguish between unresolved problems from earlier developmental stages and the normal developmental issues of adolescence. The major difference appears to be that clients are more articulate and thoughtful about the issues when they come from the adolescent stage. If the earlier developmental problems have not been solved in the therapy, however, both the client and the therapist may have difficulty distinguishing between adolescent and younger issues.

When a client is solving the problem of how to get strokes from an adolescent position, she may report that she feels fearful, but that she checks the appropriateness of the situation and goes ahead and asks for what she wants. This is quite different from the immobilizing terror felt by the Adult Child with Bonding and Separation problems, when he tries to do something direct about getting strokes.

A client reworking the Separation Stage in adolescence will be aware of not wanting to do something, and will easily learn that she can either negotiate not doing it or decide to go ahead and do it and feel okay about it. Often the only intervention that may be needed is to say, "It's okay not to want to (do it): what are you going to do?" The Adult Child who has reached this stage seldom has a problem answering the question.

Clients who are recycling the questioning of the Socialization Stage ask very adolescent questions, trying to solve the problem of not having information about normal (healthy) behavior.

We typically have extended discussions about sexuality, using materials designed for adolescent sex education. We read about how adolescents feel about sexual awakening. *Changing Bodies, Changing Lives* by Ruth Bell, and *What's Happening to Me?*, by Peter Mayle, are valuable resource books for "adolescent" Adult Children. We may share information about our own experiences of puberty, and what we might have needed.

We discuss birth control, AIDS, abortion, homosexuality and

how to decide whether or not to have intercourse with someone. Throughout these discussions, we emphasize the difference between information about physical mechanics and information about values. As therapists, we usually take an active role in the discussion, sharing our own values and the reasons we have arrived at those values. We encourage questioning, sharing and the expression of differences.

If we have been doing direct corrective parenting with a client, issues of acknowledging the client's sexuality may arise. The general message we give is, "I (the therapist) see and appreciate and approve of your sexuality. I will not be sexual with you, now or ever. As a responsible person, you have the right to decide to share your sexuality with anyone you choose. I urge you to think carefully about sexual relationships, and be sure that they do not exploit anyone involved — including you. You have the right to say *no* to *anyone*."

Clients who work on adolescent issues, after they have completed the work of earlier stages, often want to re-evaluate their career goals. Many have chosen careers that reflect their role in the family system, or that meet their parents' expectations. Pursuing these careers may have involved great investments of time, money and energy. They now face the task of deciding "what to be when I grow up" from a new and more mature perspective.

We are very cautious about supporting major career changes for "adolescent" Adult Children. Instead, we encourage exploration: taking short classes in unfamiliar subjects, doing volunteer work in the new career being considered, career counseling at the community college and occasionally professional career counseling. Some Adult Children do decide to change careers. Others rechoose their original career, but for their own mature reasons. Still others make plans to move gradually toward changes they will implement some time in the future.

Some clients use the adolescent work as an impetus to work with their family of origin, completing a separation process that they had previously been unable to manage.

Dory wrote this letter to her actively drinking alcoholic mother, who had made repeated intrusive and unwelcome attempts to interfere with Dory's life:

> Mother:
> It was an important step for me to say to you that I now understand what was going on when I was growing up. I am

*dealing with the problems that were caused by our home
situation. It took a lot of work and time for me to get to the
point of being able to say that to you. I also said to you that I
feel that no matter what situation a person grows up in, in the
end it is his responsibility to deal with that and not let it
completely cripple his life.*

*I have a whole ream of problems because you and Daddy
both were very abusive physically, emotionally and psychologically; and it is not all right with me that you two were
abusive. It has caused me no end of heartaches and
headaches in my family, marriage, business life and every
other aspect of my life. But the point to all of this is that I am
dealing with them. I am angry over the fact that you go on
ignoring that.*

*I have been needing to set some limits on our relationship
for a long time because I feel that you have in the past and
still do intrude into my life. For now, I do not choose to have
any contact or interaction with you. I feel that you have been
untruthful and manipulative with me. If we ever have any
kind of a relationship again, you will understand and respect
the fact that I will not be used by you to hurt anybody that I
love. I think that you have some very serious problems that you
need to deal with; they are not my problems. I have my own
to deal with.*

A client who is dealing with adolescent issues in preparation for
leaving treatment is encouraged to develop the nurturing part of
his Parent Ego State. Up to this point, he has been focused on
learning to nurture his own Inner Child. The experienced client
now sees the need to learn to nurture others, while continuing to
pay attention to his own needs. In the group setting, he can
practice his nurturing skills on other clients, when appropriate,
and we provide guidance and feedback about giving others what
they actually need.

We have a tradition in our groups that a client who completes
therapy may continue to attend as a volunteer therapy assistant.
There are two spaces available in each treatment group for those
who would like to assist in this way. Clients who may not be quite
finished, but for whom it would be appropriate to practice their
nuturing skills, may apprentice as assistants during the final phase
of their own treatment. They move into an older sibling position
in the therapeutic family.

People remain in this assistant capacity as long as they feel they get value out of it. Some use it as a transition time, making a very real contribution for several months, until they lose interest in the therapeutic community and find other interesting ways to spend their time. Others see it as a way of passing on some of the support they felt for their own growth. Some clients in the helping professions may stay in these positions for several years, using the experience to expand their own therapeutic skills.

Completing Treatment

When a client believes he has accomplished his goals and feels ready to leave group, we ask him to use his final three sessions to reach closure with the entire group.

He shares with the group the problems that brought him to therapy in the first place, and how those problems have been resolved. He will probably acknowledge the discovery of issues he didn't know about when he began. He describes the ways he has learned to take responsibility for his life, and can usually be fairly specific about what he is doing differently.

Group members listen carefully to see if they experience the person's recent behavior as congruent with the statements he is making. Clients and therapists give feedback, either affirming or challenging the client's self-perception, and say how they feel about the person's readiness to leave.

The developmental questionnaire is often useful as a kind of checklist, helping both the client and the therapist identify areas that have clearly changed, as well as those that could use further development. Sometimes additional work is identified at this time, and the person chooses to remain and do it. Sometimes he may choose to leave anyhow, and do the work elsewhere, at another time, or not at all.

We encourage clients to avoid leaving abruptly or against advice, but of course they always make their own choice. Clients who become sophisticated about this process sometimes define their leaving against advice as a "healthy adolescent rebellion"; they may be right.

The last two sessions provide an opportunity to review plans for the future — especially plans to create support systems to replace the familiar group supports. They also provide space and time to feel and share feelings about leaving, and to say goodbye.

When clients have completed their treatment, we are usually

both happy and sad to see them leave. They have usually become an important part of the group family, and although we wish them well, we know we will miss them. This time they leave home in a healthy way, knowing they are always welcome to come back and visit. They know that they can return for additional therapy work if they need to, and that doing so means additional growth, not failure.

CHAPTER 18

ENDINGS AND BEGINNINGS

Carl, three years into recovery from alcoholism, is in group with his pregnant wife, herself an Adult Child. After completing an intensely painful piece of therapeutic work, he sinks back into his seat, sighs and says, "I guess we're doing this so that our children won't have to."

Ending Child Abuse

The purpose of psychotherapy is to end child abuse — the abuse of the Inner Child, as well as abuse of actual children. Abuse is created and maintained as a cycle. It begins with being abused and discounted as a child, and not getting needs met as a result. In attempting to handle the damage created by the original discounting, the person learns to discount himself and others, eventually perpetuating the abuse by inflicting it on others.

Carl is now well aware of the physical and emotional abuse he suffered growing up in his alcoholic family. He is aware of many ways in which he still treats his Inner Child harshly, the way he was treated when he was a small child. He also recognizes how easy it is for him to treat others as harshly as he treats himself.

He is determined to break the cycle. He has learned that treating his Inner Child with love, understanding and respect makes him less motivated to lash out at others, and far more willing to honor their needs as well as his own.

In treatment, Carl becomes aware of the pain he has tried to avoid by abusing alcohol or by blaming others for his inner discomfort. As he exposes the still raw wounds of his Inner Child, he feels and expresses the lingering painful emotions. The growing, healthy part of him feels compassion for the child that was, and for the damaged adult that now exists.

As he works through the old pain, Carl makes room for learning new patterns of behavior. He learns to recognize his needs and communicate about them as they arise, especially to his wife. He no longer waits until he feels deprived and desperate before he lets her know he wants something. He repeatedly reminds himself his needs are: (1) natural and okay and (2) not signs of something wrong with him that has to be criticized or hidden.

He asks for and accepts nurturing from others, and learns that the pain *can* be soothed. Gradually, he is learning to love and care for those parts of his Inner Child that were discounted by his family. He knows that caring for the new baby, when it arrives, will probably stimulate even more awareness of the pain of his own Inner Child. He is committed to getting his own support, so that he will not need to try to discount the baby in order to manage his own pain.

Decisions and Redecisions

Carl is coming to recognize his Co-dependent behavior patterns as a *choice*, based on decisions he made in childhood. It is a choice in the same sense that shifting gears while driving a car is a choice; this complex process may be fully automated and unconscious, but it is still completely voluntary. The automatic process can be interrupted and changed, if necessary, by choosing to pay attention, and by deciding which parts of the pattern to correct.

In the case of Co-dependence, the behavioral choices are based on early decisions, made by the child, in a creative attempt to cope with life in a difficult environment. He may decide, for example:

1. "I won't trust anyone."
2. "No one cares what I think, feel, etc., so I'll keep it to myself."

3. "People (men, women) hurt me; I won't get close to them again."
4. "The world is a dangerous place; in order to be safe, I will do my best to control everything I can."
5. "I'll get even, if it's the last thing I do!"

These decisions, once made, become part of the child's experience of the reality of his world, and he forgets that he made them. They continue to shape his behavior and his interactions with others, however, and eventually become self-fulfilling.

Martha's alcoholic father betrays her trust often enough that she finally handles the pain by deciding never to get close to him, or any other man, again. Because this decision violates the part of her that *does* want to be close, she is in the position of having to keep reinforcing the belief that it was a good decision.

As an adult, Martha tries to express her need for closeness, but finds a series of men who betray her trust, proving over and over that her original decision was correct. Each time it happens, she says to herself, "I *knew* I shouldn't have trusted him!"

When we discuss this pattern with her, she begins to recognize that she has, in fact, been carefully *selecting* untrustworthy men to get close to, by discounting the information she gets about them early in the relationship.

The Adult Child is in the position of trying to manage an adult life on the basis of the decisions made by a mistreated child. Sometimes the pain of carrying out these life-repressing decisions becomes so overwhelming that the person tries to self-medicate it. The resulting addictive or compulsive substitute behaviors typically make things even more unmanageable. Even though he is usually unaware of the source of his own dysfunctional patterns, he recognizes that something isn't working, and comes for help.

In therapy, *Carl*, like many Adult Children, first struggled with blame, alternately blaming himself and blaming others for his unhappiness. Once he was able to stop the blaming, he began to see things differently: "Things happened to me when I was small and helpless, and I *decided* to live my life in a certain way. I am no longer small and helpless (even though I often feel that way), and I can *change my decisions* and live differently."

When substitute behavior patterns are created during the first two years of life, the concept of the child making a choice or a decision is more of a metaphor than a literal description of the process. For treatment purposes, however, the metaphor of choice is far more supportive of the client doing something about his problems than the idea that he was a helpless victim.

A child whose needs are not met in his dysfunctional family still has the needs, and he eventually works out the best solutions he can find — the substitute behaviors — to express those needs and get *some* response. Even though the child has a limited ability to understand what is happening, and a limited range of choices available, the creation of the substitute behavior is best understood as a decision. As an adult, he now has the power to create different experiences for his Inner Child than those he originally had to react to.

The limiting decisions, made when the child was in distress, need to be changed. Because the original decisions were made by a child, the adult must involve his Inner Child in the redecision process. He must allow the Inner Child to reexperience the pain and unhappiness he was trying to manage when he made the original decision.

In order for the Inner Child to be willing to face such pain again, he must have some promise that it will be worth it, that his needs *can* be met. **When the Adult Child relearns the healthy cycle of feeling needs, expressing them and having those needs met, the Inner Child can be reassured that he *will* always be nurtured by the grown-up self. In the face of this information, it is possible for the Inner Child to make new decisions.**

Forgiveness

When his grief and rage are fully expressed, the Adult Child may decide to forgive his parents. As the pain is worked through, and the old decisions drop away, the Adult Child slowly emerges with a sense of Self, an awareness of his own boundaries and a new self-confidence. As he reowns and accepts the disowned parts of himself, he may develop compassion for the damaged young people his parents were when he was a child.

Connie had worked hard to discover and express the anger she felt at her mother for the way she had been treated as a three-year-old. However, she seemed to have gotten stuck in the anger, and was continuing to focus her attention on how much her mother was to blame for everything wrong in Connie's life. We suggested that she try a new perspective.

We asked Connie how old her mother had been when Connie was three. Connie realized, with surprise, that mother *then* was younger than Connie *now*. Connie was encouraged to imagine herself at her current age, 34, having a conversation with her 28-year-old mother.

Connie found she could approach that image of her mother from the position of a mature friend who had been studying parenting skills. She discovered that Mom was unsure of herself, under pressure, trying hard and doing the very best she could. Mother was grateful for grown-up Connie's support in learning to parent little Connie. When Connie completed that imaginary conversation, she finally accepted her mother as a real person, with real strengths and weaknesses.

Several months later, Connie's mother came out to visit. Connie was amazed at how her relationship with her mother changed. Instead of resentfully manipulating her mother, trying to get approval and love, Connie found herself appreciating her mother as another woman she truly enjoyed being with. Her first thought, "Mother has changed," was quickly replaced with the realization that she had forgiven her mother for being human instead of perfect.

As Connie forgives her own mother, she also begins to recognize how she has been trying to parent her own children with her damaged Inner Child, the part of herself that thought she was supposed to take care of others — and resented it.

Instead of berating herself, as she has done in the past, she grieves. She has a conversation with her Inner Child, and acknowledges, "I know you did the best you could with what you knew; I forgive you. It's not your job to take care of the children; it's mine, and I know more about how to do it now."

She turns to us saying, "I have lots of work to do to help the children break the cycle, too." As she continues her own therapy work with us, her children are doing better. As Connie grows in maturity and self-confidence, she is gradually reversing the damage she created by the way she parented them.

Several years after **Pegg** completed treatment, her mother cancelled a promised visit on very short notice. Pegg wrote:

Disappointments

Disappointed again and the hot angry tears flow —
I acknowledge the feelings and the sadness.
Slowly I let go and begin the process of healing

*Knowing, you are what you are and have little awareness of
the hurting I have inside
And yet I know that I still love you.*

                                                        Pegg Hawkins

Spirituality

In the process of healing the Inner Child, the Adult Child must first learn to focus on her own wants and needs. She gradually expands her awareness to include the needs and wants of others, and develops a more and more realistic picture of the workings of the world around her. As the Inner Child heals, it is easier to see the love and beauty in another, and mature, loving relationships are established. This awareness and appreciation of others expands, naturally, into a concern for the larger community, perhaps for the world as a whole. Somewhere in this process of growth and expansion, a natural interest in spiritual growth often occurs.

A mature interest in spiritual development should not be confused with a regressive flight into mystical or religious experiences as a way to avoid pain. Adult Chidlren who never successfully bonded with another human being often seek to bond with and give themselves to "God" in much the same way an infant attempts to bond symbiotically with an all-knowing and all-powerful parent. From this position, they approach God from the point of view that says, "I'm helpless, and you are here to take care of me completely. If you don't, I'll be angry at you."

Adult Children in this position are quite vulnerable to charismatic religious and quasireligious organizations that promise oneness and bliss. This kind of situation almost always leads to disillusionment. It promises the bliss of unity without acknowledging or working through the pain of abandonment that the Adult Child wants to deny anyhow.

Although they may, for a while, experience some kind of connectedness with others, it is superficial, at best, and always comes at the expense of giving up individuality. The Co-dependent pattern is reinforced, not cured. When the artificial bliss breaks down, the reality of earning a living and relating to others is still there. The pain of not having adequate coping skills may be even worse than before.

When Adult Children feel drawn to explore spirituality as a way of recovery, it is important that they find a balanced path, one that focuses on *both* a "Higher Power" *and* individual responsibility. The Twelve-Step programs of AA, Al-Anon and other support groups for people with addictive and compulsive behaviors, are excellent examples of balance. These programs place great emphasis upon finding a "Power greater than ourselves" and turning one's life over to "God as we understand Him". At the same time, they also emphasize self-understanding and taking action to make amends for any harm done to others.

All adults need to balance their needs for attachment and for individuation; these needs recur throughout life. Many religious, mystical and spiritual disciplines describe a world view in which "We are all one with God", all connected to and part of one another and the Universe. The next cycle of growth for many recovering Adult Children seems to be in this area. There appears to be another recycling of the need to attach, in order to develop further. This new form of attachment also seems to include the necessity to more fully discover one's own unique individuality. This is the next developmental task. Humans are built never to stop growing.

There are many levels of spiritual development, and most of them are not visible at the beginning of the journey. Because the spiritual approaches appear to emphasize unity and oneness, it is easy to mistake a spiritual path for a call to abandon one's individuality. For this reason, guides, teachers and mentors are necessary to help us keep from getting lost. Someone who has already traveled the path is in a good position to help us maintain our balance while exploring.

Endings And Beginnings

Therapy ends when the Adult Child makes her own life therapeutic. Therapy is no longer necessary when she has learned to acknowledge and appreciate all of the parts of herself. Her Inner Child is no longer desperately needy, and no longer intrudes on her ability to meet her current needs. She loves and accepts herself, and finds that there is space to love and accept others easily. Healthy relationships develop. She no longer needs others to "take care of her" because she is dysfunctional. She has the tools to easily handle the ordinary problems of living as they arise.

In observing the healing process of many of our clients, we notice a change in their understanding of God. The Adult Child who completes the process of separation and individuation seems to develop a less self-centered and more mature understanding of God and spirituality. He comes to accept his own responsibility for creating and maintaining a balance between the great polarities — oneness and separateness, spirituality and "hardheaded" realism, logic and intuition, male and female, etc. He begins to see that these are not sides to choose, or competing versions of Truth, but complementary aspects of a complex reality. As therapy ends, a whole new cycle of growth begins.

By the time Adult Children can pursue spirituality in a serious, mature way, the pain of growing up in a dysfunctional family is past. They have become strong in the broken places. Ordinary problems are handled easily and effectively. Relationships are usually joyful and growth-supporting. They often take leadership positions helping others in the process of recovery, and make important contributions to the world.

Two and a half years after completing treatment, *Jenny* writes us (excerpts):

> *School last year (a major Eastern university) was a wonderful first year experience. I ended with an A+ average; I received almost a full scholarship from (the University) as a result for this year, and have moved into a very nice (University-owned) studio apartment. One of my main reasons for moving up here is to develop a social life.*
>
> *I am taking many wonderful courses this year, and I am doing something really scary — entering (the University's) writing program, one of the best, and the toughest, in the country. Yes, I am petrified and excited at the same time.*
>
> *I find myself in a sort of "crossing-over" stage in my life. All the work I've done up until now has seemingly been coalescing over these last two years. Though I still often feel like an awkward kid, I can feel and see a maturation in myself, and I am going through a period of reclaiming former creative sources of power and strength. Achieving what I have, making things happen, etc., has been a real practice of what I have learned, and a sort of testing ground to see where I am and where I need to go personally. Many things came up for me over the trip to Africa — feelings of isolation and inadequacy — many old memories and feelings. But I*

think that I am very capable of finding really good, safe healthy places for me to work this stuff through in a workshop environment, where I would have the opportunity to clear myself, get support and information, and then process it on my own or with friends. I seem to be entering into a new level of relationship with others. A new, deeper level of connection and intimacy seems to be knocking at my door. I seem to have to answer such calls, however much I may kick and scream.

I really am doing quite well . . .

Love to you both,

Jenny

Growing up takes time, and so does reclaiming a Happy Childhood. We hope this book is a useful road map for therapists and Adult Children on the road to recovery. The healing process is not linear. Sometimes months of hard work seem to produce no change, and suddenly major changes occur almost overnight. The rewards are worth the journey.

APPENDIX I

Self-Assessment Questionnaire

Name _____

Please respond to the following statements by circling the number that most closely describes how accurate the statement is for you.

	Never		Seldom		Sometimes		Often		Always
1. I know when my body needs something (food, air, water, rest, etc.).	1	2	3	4	5	6	7	8	9	10
2. I am effective about making sure my environment supports my physical needs.	1	2	3	4	5	6	7	8	9	10
3. I know when I need strokes.	1	2	3	4	5	6	7	8	9	10
4. I am comfortable in new situations.	1	2	3	4	5	6	7	8	9	10
5. I can try out new things without getting in trouble or hurting myself.	1	2	3	4	5	6	7	8	9	10
6. I am comfortable selecting what I like and don't like in new situations.	1	2	3	4	5	6	7	8	9	10
7. I can enjoy myself by exploring something new.	1	2	3	4	5	6	7	8	9	10
8. I feel independent and autonomous.	1	2	3	4	5	6	7	8	9	10
9. When I make decisions, I count myself and others equally.	1	2	3	4	5	6	7	8	9	10

(Appendix I — Self-Assessment Questionnaire Continued)

	Never	Seldom	Sometimes	Often	Always
10. I am comfortable sharing my ideas and opinions with others who have ideas of their own, even if their ideas differ from mine.	1 2	3 4	5 6	7 8	9 10
11. I am comfortable about the ways in which I am different from others.	1 2	3 4	5 6	7 8	9 10
12. I am comfortable about the ways in which I am similar to others.	1 2	3 4	5 6	7 8	9 10
13. I am able to be vocal and stubborn in opposing things I think are destructive.	1 2	3 4	5 6	7 8	9 10
14. I am comfortable asking questions when I don't understand or want to know something.	1 2	3 4	5 6	7 8	9 10
15. I can recognize and acknowledge other people's feelings.	1 2	3 4	5 6	7 8	9 10
16. I have the ability to find out what others feel, when I don't know.	1 2	3 4	5 6	7 8	9 10
17. I can confront others when I see problems in what they are doing, saying or feeling.	1 2	3 4	5 6	7 8	9 10
18. I can tell when to give up on something that isn't working.	1 2	3 4	5 6	7 8	9 10
19. I am willing to feel sadness and grief when I have to let go of something that was important to me.	1 2	3 4	5 6	7 8	9 10

(Appendix I — Self-Assessment Questionnaire Continued)

	Never	Seldom		Sometimes		Often		Always
20. I am comfortable learning how to do new things that I didn't know how to do before.	1	2	3	4	5	6	7	8	9	10
21. I do things as well as they need to be done.	1	2	3	4	5	6	7	8	9	10
22. I finish things that need to be finished.	1	2	3	4	5	6	7	8	9	10
23. I can recognize and communicate about the reasons for my values and beliefs.	1	2	3	4	5	6	7	8	9	10
24. I can recognize and understand that others have different reasons for their values and beliefs.	1	2	3	4	5	6	7	8	9	10
25. I am comfortable negotiating openly with others to satisfy our needs and wants.	1	2	3	4	5	6	7	8	9	10
26. I recognize and am comfortable with the fact that I am connected to other people.	1	2	3	4	5	6	7	8	9	10
27. I can be interdependent with others without sacrificing my own autonomy.	1	2	3	4	5	6	7	8	9	10

©Jonathan B. Weiss and Laurie A. Weiss, 1983.

Bibliography

Bell, R. **Changing Bodies, Changing Lives.** New York: Random House, 1980.

Berne, E. **Transactional Analysis In Psychotherapy.** New York: Grove Press, 1961.

Berne, E. **Games People Play.** New York: Grove Press, 1964.

Berne, E. **What Do You Say After You Say Hello?** New York: Grove Press, 1970.

Black, C. **It Will Never Happen To Me.** Denver, Colorado: M.A.C. Publications Division, 1982.

Cassidy, J., and Rimbeaux, B. C. **Juggling For The Compleat Klutz.** Stanford, California: Klutz Press, 1977.

Cermak, T. **Diagnosing And Treating Co-dependence.** Minneapolis: Johnson Institute, 1986.

Dwinnel, L., and Middleton-Moz, J. **After The Tears.** Pompano Beach, Florida: Health Communications, 1986.

Fisher, R., and Urey, W. **Getting To Yes.** Boston: Houghton Mifflin, 1981.

Forward, S. **Men Who Hate Women And The Women Who Love Them.** New York: Bantam Books, 1986.

Gravitz, H. L., and Bowden, J. D. **Guide To Recovery: A Book For Adult Children Of Alcoholics.** Holmes Beach, Florida: Learning Publications, 1985.

Harris, T. **I'm OK — You're OK.** New York: Harper & Row, 1967.

Justice, B. **Who Gets Sick?** Houston: Peak Press, 1987.

Kaplan, L. **Oneness And Separateness: From Infant To Individual.** New York: Simon & Schuster, 1978.

Kiley, D. **The Peter Pan Syndrome.** New York: Dodd, Mead, 1983.

Leman, K. **The Birth Order Book.** New York: Dell, 1985.

Levin, P. **Becoming The Way We Are: A Transactional Guide to Personal Development.** Deerfield Beach, Florida: Health Communications, 1988.

Masterson, W. **Psychotherapy Of The Borderline Adult.** New York: Brunner/Mazel, 1976.

Mayle, P. **Where Did I Come From?** Secaucus, New Jersey: Lyle Stuart, 1975.

Mayle, P. **What's Happening To Me?** Secaucus, New Jersey: Lyle Stuart, 1975.

Miller, A. **The Drama Of The Gifted Child.** New York: Basic Books, 1981.

Miller, A. **For Your Own Good.** New York: Farrar Straus Giroux, 1983.

Norwood, R. **Women Who Love Too Much.** Los Angeles: Tarcher/St. Martin's Press, 1985.

Paine-Gerne, K. "Adult Children of Alcoholics: Implications for Treatment." In *AHP Perspective* Aug. - Sept., 1986: 4.

Schaef, A. W. **Co-dependence: Misunderstood, Mistreated.** Minneapolis, Winston Press, 1986.

Schaef, A. W. **When Society Becomes An Addict.** San Francisco: Harper & Row, 1987.

Schiff, J. L., et al. **The Cathexis Reader.** New York: Harper & Row, 1975.

Steiner, C. **Scripts People Live.** New York: Grove Press, 1974.

Subby, R. "Inside The Chemically Dependent Marriage: Denial And Manipulation." in **Co-Dependency: An Emerging Issue.** Pompano Beach, Florida: Health Communications, 1984.

Wegscheider-Cruse, S. **Choicemaking.** Pompano Beach, Florida: Health Communications, 1985.

Woititz, J. **Adult Children Of Alcoholics.** Pompano Beach, Florida: Health Communications, 1983.

Woititz, J. **Struggle For Intimacy.** Pompano Beach, Florida: Health Communications, 1985.

SUPPLEMENTAL READING*

Babcock, D., and Keepers, T. **Raising Kids OK**. New York: Grove Press, 1976.

Bradshaw, J. **Bradshaw On: The Family — A Revolutionary Way Of Self-Discovery**. Pompano Beach, FL: Health Communications, 1988.

Cermak, T. **A Primer On Adult Children Of Alcoholics**. Pompano Beach, Florida: Health Communications, 1985.

Clarke, J. **Self-Esteem: A Family Affair**. Minneapolis, Minnesota: Winston Press, 1978.

Goulding, R.L., and Goulding, M.M. **The Power Is In The Patient: A TA/Gestalt Approach To Psychotherapy**. San Francisco: TA Press, 1978.

Levin, P. **Cycles of Power: A User's Guide To The Seven Stages Of Life**. Deerfield Beach, FL: Health Communications, 1988.

Schiff, J. **All My Children**. New York: M. Evans, 1970.

Wegscheider, S. **Another Chance: Hope And Health For The Alcoholic Family**. Palo Alto, CA: Science and Behavior Books, 1981.

Weiss, L., and Weiss, J. "The Good Child Syndrome." in E. Stern (ed.), **TA: The State Of The Art, A European Contribution**. Dordrecht, Holland: Foris, 1984.

Weiss, L. "Getting To 'No' And Beyond." in L. Rosewater and L. Walker (eds.), **Handbook Of Feminist Therapy: Women's Issues In Psychotherapy**. New York: Springer, 1985.

*A complete selection of titles relating to Transactional Analysis is available from Trans Pubs, 1259 El Camino Real, Suite 209, Menlo Park, CA 94025, (415) 325-6487.

Other Books By ...

HEALTH COMMUNICATIONS, INC.

Enterprise Center
3201 Southwest 15th Street
Deerfield Beach, FL 33442
Phone: 800-851-9100

ADULT CHILDREN OF ALCOHOLICS
Janet Woititz
Over a year on The New York Times Best Seller list,this book is the primer
on Adult Children of Alcoholics.
ISBN 0-932194-15-X $6.95

STRUGGLE FOR INTIMACY
Janet Woititz
Another best seller, this book gives insightful advice on learning to love
more fully.
ISBN 0-932194-25-7 $6.95

DAILY AFFIRMATIONS: For Adult Children of Alcoholics
Rokelle Lerner
These positive affirmations for every day of the year paint a mental picture
of your life as you choose it to be.
ISBN 0-932194-27-3 $6.95

*CHOICEMAKING: For Co-dependents, Adult Children and Spirituality
Seekers* — Sharon Wegscheider-Cruse
This useful book defines the problems and solves them in a positive way.
ISBN 0-932194-26-5 $9.95

LEARNING TO LOVE YOURSELF: Finding Your Self-Worth
Sharon Wegscheider-Cruse
"Self-worth is a choice, not a birthright", says the author as she shows us
how we can choose positive self-esteem.
ISBN 0-932194-39-7 $7.95

LET GO AND GROW: Recovery for Adult Children
Robert Ackerman
An in-depth study of the different characteristics of adult children of
alcoholics with guidelines for recovery.
ISBN 0-932194-51-6 $8.95

LOST IN THE SHUFFLE: The Co-dependent Reality
Robert Subby
A look at the unreal rules the co-dependent lives by and the way out of the
dis-eased reality.
ISBN 0-932194-45-1 $8.95

New Books . . .
from Health Communications

BRADSHAW ON: THE FAMILY: A Revolutionary Way of Self-Discovery
John Bradshaw
The host of the nationally televised series of the same name shows us how families can be healed and we as individuals can realize our full potential.
ISBN 0-932194-54-0 $9.95

HEALING THE CHILD WITHIN: Discovery and recovery for Adult Children of Dysfunctional Families — Charles Whitfield
Dr. Whitfield defines, describes and discovers how we can reach our Child Within to heal and nurture our woundedness.
ISBN 0-932194-40-0 $8.95

WHISKY'S SONG: An Explicit Story of Surviving in an Alcoholic Home
Mitzi Chandler
A beautiful but brutal story of growing up where violence and neglect are everyday occurrences conveys a positive message of survival and love.
ISBN 0-932194-42-7 $6.95

New Books on Spiritual Recovery . . .
from Health Communications

THE JOURNEY WITHIN: A Spiritual Path to Recovery
Ruth Fishel
This book will lead you from your dysfunctional beginnings to the place within where renewal occurs.
ISBN 0-932194-41-9 $8.95

LEARNING TO LIVE IN THE NOW: 6-Week Personal Plan To Recovery
Ruth Fishel
The author gently introduces you to the valuable healing tools of meditation, positive creative visualization and affirmations.
ISBN 0-932194-62-1 $7.95

GENESIS: Spirituality in Recovery for Co-dependents
by Julie D. Bowden and Herbert L. Gravitz
A self-help spiritual program for adult children of trauma, an in-depth look at "turning it over" and "letting go".
ISBN 0-932194-56-7 $6.95

GIFTS FOR PERSONAL GROWTH AND RECOVERY
Wayne Kritsberg
Gifts for healing which include journal writing, breathing, positioning and meditation.
ISBN 0-932194-60-5 $6.95